Learning
to
Avoid
Unintended
Consequences

Leonard A. Renier

ISBN 0-7414-1734-0

Published by:

INFINITY
PUBLISHING.COM
519 West Lancaster Avenue
Haverford, PA 19041-1413
Info@buybooksontheweb.com
www.buybooksontheweb.com
Toll-free (877) BUY BOOK
Local Phone (610) 520-2500
Fax (610) 519-0261

Printed in the United States of America

Printed on Recycled Paper

Published October 2003

ACKNOWLEDGMENTS

There are several people who have influenced my life and thought process, and who have helped me find the energy to write my opinions. My wife, Janice, gave me support to start and complete this task. My kids supported my seminars and gave encouragement.

The people who expanded my knowledge in my business played an important role in my life. Don Blanton, founder of Money Trax, absolutely changed my career. His knowledge is the basis for many of my thoughts. I would recommend anyone in the financial business to look him up. Also Paul Kinnel, who helped me establish systems into my business.

From everyday standpoint, one of my associates, Grecia Souffront, who encouraged me, supported me, and edited this book. Nothing can replace the nice things she, and all the other aforementioned individuals, have done for me.

DISCLAIMER

CONTENTS

THE THOUGHT PROCESS

WHO SHOULD READ THIS

The goal of this book is to create a defining moment in the way you think about money. That defining moment will occur with your understanding of the *Efficiency of Money*. The concepts that will be discussed are simple yet effective methods of reducing and/or eliminating financial transfers of your wealth that you make everyday, unknowingly and unnecessarily. Your savings, by utilizing some of these concepts, could be staggering. If properly suited, this knowledge could create more financial options and opportunities for you in the future.

The goal is also to help you through a thought process that will make you think a layer deeper when it comes to your money. Your financial knowledge is being controlled by others. They feed you enough knowledge to play the financial game but never enough to win. Financially, we are devoid of new ideas and have become brain dead in our everyday financial dealings. We have become pallbearers for our money.

We have been defeated by banks, the government, taxation, credit cards interest, automobile financing, mortgage companies, and overall, personal debt. The evolution of transferring your wealth away to others is based on their ability to create situations, control the outcomes, and profit from it. Eliminating as many of these transfers as you can will change your life.

Everyone can profit from reading this book. It will be more effective for some than others. If you match up to just four of the nine following criteria, this book will change the way you think about money: Strong household income; Owner of a home valued over $100,000; Married; Children; Participant in a retirement plan; Business owner; Executive or management level professional; College educated, and; 35 years of age or older.

If you have come close to matching four or more of these criteria, or will in the near future, you must read this book. When you do, you will be financially brought back to life. If you can accomplish this without spending one more dime than you are already spending, would you do it?

This book is NOT about helping you pick stocks or mutual funds or how to cheat on your taxes. It is NOT about offshore banking, financial pyramid schemes, or creating red flags for the IRS. It is NOT about clipping coupons or buying cheap products or living on a minuscule budget. It is quite the opposite.

Knowledge is power. Knowledge can be time-consuming and expensive (the cost of this book). Now, consider the cost of not knowing something. There lieth the lesson.

INTENT

This book is intended to help you understand *The Thought Process*, identify *The Transfers*, and recognize *The Creators of the Transfers*.

THE THOUGHT PROCESS

Here we try to uncover flaws in some of the conventional financial wisdom. A lot of this wisdom is misguided. It lies somewhere between opinion and fact, between myth and reality. The opinion and myth portion of this knowledge can create confusion. It is important to be able to identify what is opinion and myth in your own personal financial lives. It is here where unintended financial consequences occur. The fact and reality is that with the basic wisdom we have been given we will ultimately transfer large portions of our wealth away to others. The people feeding us this wisdom are the benefactors of these wealth transfers. If they can control your thought process, they can control the outcome. It is time to uncover some of the consequences we must pay for when we follow this advice. One must realize that the upcoming events, such as the demographics of the country and the changes that will be necessary, will affect all of us financially. You must develop a financial thought process that will eliminate or reduce transfers of your wealth.

IDENTIFYING TRANSFERS

Being able to identify the transfers of your wealth is important. We want to take a look at ten of the most common transfers that may affect you. You may be in a position to reduce some of these transfers right away. You will find though that there are unintended financial consequences attached to all of them. Once a transfer is recognized it is important to learn to recapture as many of those dollars that you are unknowingly and unnecessarily giving away. In these transfers you will be able to see the opinions and myths for what they really are: profits for others. Recapturing these transfers will change your life and give you more financial control and freedom. You may discover that there are solutions when dealing with these transfers. That defining moment will change the way you think about your money.

WHO IS CREATING THESE TRANSFERS?

Finally, we will address who is causing these transfers of your wealth. When you identify these perpetrators you will be able to deal with them more effectively. These are the people and institutions that create situations, control the outcomes, and profit from it. In the past, we obtained financial advice from these sources. Many times we are led down a narrow path that they control only to find that the outcome isn't quite what you thought it would be. You might discover that the financial solutions they provided for you may profit them more than it does you. Their thought processes may create more unintended consequences for you in the form of higher taxes, more fees, and higher interest rates.

URGENCY

The vast majority of people are troubled and confused about the economy. They are bombarded by the media, bullied by sales people, and bewildered by the millions of things they feel they need to know to survive in this financial jungle. Over the past few years they have seen all the investment lessons they learned in the 80's, the 90's and beyond fail them. They know they can't live much longer on 5% rates of return and yet they are scared and hesitant to make crucial decisions. To make things worse, right now 90 million Americans are faced with the most critical investment challenges of their lives.[1]

We are going to shed some light on this darkness. We will break these problems down and analyze them carefully. Then you will have a clear view of choices open to you. You will feel more confident and prepared to make financial decisions.

MORE THAN ONE SOLUTION

Traditional financial thinking of the past has always emphasized the rate of return on our investments. The faster you want your money to grow, the greater the risk you would have to take. Many words have been spoken and written about risk tolerance and risk management, so I'm not going to rehash popular current financial thinking. I do think the element of risk is important, but only to the extent that if you didn't have to take a risk, and could receive positive rates of return, would you pursue that course of planning?

It is a popular belief that the only way to make your money grow is to get higher rates of return. Every time I hear "higher rate of return," I ask a question: "Who is at risk, you or the one making the recommendation?" There is another way to increase your wealth without the worry of risk. It is called

---

[1] Frank Maselli, *Seminars - The Emotional Dynamic* (Kearney, Nevada: Morris Publishing, 1996)

the *Efficiency of Money*. Now I'm not talking about strict budgets, buying off-brands, and doing without. I'm talking about the complete opposite. You should have the finer things in life and enjoy them. The only thing stopping you from achieving this is money, and more precisely, *transferred* money. We unknowingly and unnecessarily transfer away most of our wealth and it's out of control. Have you ever stood in a supermarket line with that ½ gallon of ice cream you forgot to get for the kid's birthday party, only to have the person in front of you contest the cost of one of their items? The argument starts out polite enough over this $.10 difference in cost, and escalates into a conflict between the store manager and a cell phone call to the shopper's attorney. Finally, it is resolved with some U. N. intervention. Meanwhile, your fudge swirl delight is dripping down your arm onto your new shoes. The shopper leaves the store victorious in battle, proud and happy, eager to share the success of their confrontation with all who will listen.

Did I get off track there? Not really. If we had the passion and the knowledge to confront the transfers of our wealth, we would surprisingly win most of the battles. Instead of a $.10 victory, the savings could be in the thousands of dollars with no risk of loss.

There are ten major transfers of your wealth. We will be discussing some of them in great detail. It will take some encouragement by me for you to begin thinking a layer deeper than you are accustomed to. Remember, the purpose of taking you a layer deeper is not to uncover defects in your thinking, but to expand your thought process through knowledge so you will be able to make better financial decisions. Without this process, you may suffer unintended consequences in your financial future.

When we are finished, you will have a defining moment

in the way you think about money. You will have a greater appreciation of opportunities that you didn't have before. Let's face it, finance companies, banks, the government, credit card companies, mortgage companies, etc. are all standing in line for their share of your money. Where do you and your family stand in this line? At the end! We will change this. However, in order to change this, your thought process must change.

POPULAR BELIEFS

About 6,000 months ago, it was a widely accepted scientific fact that our planet, the Earth, was flat. About 600 months ago, my father was told he would probably retire to two-thirds of his income, thus, he would be in a lower tax bracket. About 60 months ago, we were told of such enormous surpluses controlled by the federal government that our society would prosper from increased government programs. All of these beliefs turned out not to be true. Tax reform acts designed to relieve tax burdens on the public, actually resulted in the government collecting <u>more</u> revenue than ever from its citizens, you and I. The shell game of lowering tax rates while eliminating deductions has been very profitable for the government. Back in our grandparents' day, Social Security was the save-all safety net they needed in lieu of the lack of retirement plans. Although well intended it was the first step of a long journey of dependency on the government. The 16th Amendment of the U. S. Constitution allowed taxation of income of its citizens.[2] Originally, the idea of income tax was

---

[2]U. S. Constitution, Amendment XVI.

ruled unconstitutional in the 1890's. Article 1, Section 9 of the Constitution states clearly that no direct tax "shall be laid, unless in proportion to the census or enumeration herein before directed to be taken."[3] The 16th Amendment gave new powers to the federal government that conflicted with the 10th Amendment that reserves any other power, other than stated in the Constitution, to the individual states.[4] In 1913, 400 pages of tax law were created. Today almost 47,000 pages of tax codes and rulings exist. We will continue, later on, to look into transfers of your wealth to the government, created by the government.

Four score and several years ago our forefathers brought forth onto this continent a new notion, that all men are created equal. . . when it comes to taxes. Once again, most of the popular beliefs have been handed down generation to generation, father to son, mother to daughter with very little effort on studying these beliefs. Now we are at a point where there is confusion between myth, opinion, and fact. Misinformation has caused all of us enormous amounts of lost money, in the form of transfers that we've made unknowingly and unnecessarily.

The government isn't the only player trying to share your wealth. Banks are notorious for dipping into your wallet. One rule of the bank you must understand. If a bank is late on doing something it's called a "process." If you are late with the bank it's called a "fee." Most recently, a bank charged me a $360.00 fee for not doing something - for not setting up an escrow account for a mortgage. Think about it, $360.00 for

---

[3]U.S. Constitution, Article 1, Section 9.

[4]U.S. Constitution, Amendment X.

doing nothing. When they were questioned about this fee, they said it was simply part of the process of the mortgage. The process of setting up nothing. When asked where that money goes . . . well, the silence was deafening. I could actually hear the crickets chirping.

Besides mortgages, other spinoffs of their creations, such as credit cards, home loans, auto loans, ATM's, checking accounts, saving accounts, and certificates of deposit (CD) all create fees. Late fees, early withdrawal fees, minimum balance fees, debit fees, and in some cases, a fee to talk to a teller. On credit cards, its almost the goal that you be a couple of days late on your payments. Late fees are big business, and so are charge-offs from bad debts. To create higher possibilities of late payments, the billing cycle has been shortened. Instead of sending out your billing 14 days before the due date, it is sent out 10 days before the due date, and the due date is probably on a weekend. Wouldn't it be terrific if **we** could be the bank? If you are interested in creating your own personal bank and eliminating regular commercial banks from your life, you must read on.

IF SOMETHING YOU THOUGHT TO BE TRUE, WASN'T TRUE. . .

It is difficult to get the right solution when you start out with the wrong premise. If we center ourselves in a false belief system, we become what we believe. An example of that false belief system in one particular case existed until 1954, just about 600 months ago. It was common belief that no human could run a mile in less than four minutes and live to tell about it. Medically, it was believed at that time that to attempt to run a mile in less than four minutes would bring about certain disaster to the human body. No one in the history of mankind was ever timed running a sub-four minute mile. . . no one, that is, until Fred Banister. On a sunny Saturday morning, the young Englishman defeated a belief system and certain death by running one mile in 3:59:40. Now recently, record performances in the mile have been run in 3:47:48, and 6 to 10 times daily someone runs a sub-four minute mile.

The real lesson here is that our lives are shaped by this simple fact: We become what we believe. Financially, we assume things to be true that are not, simply because others told us they were true. Many financial organizations stand to profit from these misconceptions, since they create a fear that if you don't use their services, you will fail. Their real fear is, that you don't need them. They're the ones who created the idea that change is bad.

BECOME A TABLE DANCER

Go home, walk into your kitchen, what do you see? You have probably been in that room thousands of times. Now do something different, stand on your kitchen table. Look around. You will see the room from a different perspective. You will notice things you have never seen before even though physically, nothing has changed. I want to challenge you to stand on your table of knowledge about your finances. Take a new look around. Now, do you see things differently? Without more knowledge and different perspectives about what you are doing financially, possibly not. But by learning new ideas and concepts about money, your view will change. If something you thought to be true wasn't true, when would you want to know about it? Right away? It still amazes me that some people continue down the same path, knowing it was wrong for them but refuse to change because they would have to confront their mistakes. But the decisions to follow these losing financial strategies were based on limited knowledge. Had they been given more knowledge, their lives would have changed. In order to change, we must study how, when, and where we received all of our financial knowledge.

We can learn a lot about what we know about finances by studying where we get our information. First, we learned from our parents, who learned from their parents and so on and so on. From our parents we learned the basic principles of saving money, but these lessons were loaded with an enormous amount of fear. Going back two generations, we see their experiences of stock market crashes, bank failures, business closings, massive unemployment, depression, families losing homes and farms, and world wars left very little to be positive about. People living in this era were in the survival mode because there was no other mode to be in. What, if any, positive lessons were branded into their kids? Work hard, save what you can, and pay off your house as fast as you can so you don't lose it.

The next generation cherished their hard earned lessons, fought off a couple of wars, and came home to raise families with a new reassurance that the government would provide Social Security - a retirement income for them. Unions became forefront in industry, adopting ideas from the railroads and establishing retirement benefits for workers. There was great expansion in American society. The new learned financial lesson: Don't worry we will take care of you. If you can't take care of yourself, don't worry, we will help provide for you (social programs). This was great, but it created dependency.

Unintended Consequences:
The Thought Process

Lessons learned? Finish high school, get a good job with benefits, and pay the house off as soon as you can. By the time my generation came along, the lessons were go to college, get a good job with benefits, save what you can, pay off your house as soon as you can, and retire early.

The generation we are now producing have some real financial lessons they can sink their teeth into: Have your parents pay for college, complete a four year degree in six years, get a job you like, live with your parents as long as you can, encourage your parents to pay off their house and accumulate a nice retirement fund, and then commit them into a home as soon as you can and take over their money. Oh, I forgot, retire now and become a day trader.

Of course, to some extent, I'm kidding. . .or does some of this sound familiar? Did I forget to mention all those great financial lessons the banks taught us, all those money saving lessons from the government, all those hours accountants spent teaching how to create wealth? How about the money lessons in personal finance classes in college? All you got when you graduated was a lot of debt and an unbalanced checkbook. Ahh, success! With all that financial support you get from these groups, you can count on one thing: controlled failure.

To become successful financially, all you have to do is shed some of the historical bias which we have been branded with. The solution is a thought process not a product purchase. We will teach you new concepts and knowledge so you can make better financial decisions. You will have a defining moment in the way you think about money. Are you willing to change?

DEMOGRAPH X

Without understanding the demographics of our society, any attempt to financially plan our future will be doomed and filled with unintended consequences. My spelling of *demographX* with an "X" represents a missing factor. The "X" represents all the necessary changes that will have to be made by the government in order for it to survive. This will dramatically effect our personal retirement wealth. Demographics have been basically ignored in most financial planning. This will create major flaws in any future financial projections, and could leave us exposed to many financial hazards.

3,000 DAYS

In 3,000 days almost two-thirds of the now-working population will be 60 years old or older. In 3,000 days there will be less working taxpayers and more retirees living off government social programs. The cost of these government programs will greatly increase simply by the rising number of participants in them. According to the 2000 U. S. Census, since 1990, there was a 12% increase in people 65 years of age or older. It is estimated that by the year 2040, the elderly will represent 20.7% of the total population. Since 1990, the fastest growing segment of the population were people between the ages of 90 and 94, having increased by 44%. Overall, the number of people between the ages of 80 and 94 increased 25.7% in the same time frame. A 65-year old woman in the United States as of the year 2000 could expect to live another 19.2 years, and a man of the same age could expect to live another 16.3 years. In 1900, the average life expectancy was only 47.3 years.

We must also factor in that these programs increase in cost every year just to maintain them. The remaining one-third of the work force will not only have to support government social programs, they will also still want an increased standard of living for themselves. At what cost will this be achievable? Surely, their taxation level will be enormous. Not only will there be trouble with the idea of preserving their own financial future, they must also provide for the government's financial future. Even with very clear warning signs, the government continues in its record levels of spending. The debt of the nation continues to spiral upward, out of control, for future generations to figure out. Lets face it, the only power our Federal Representatives have is their ability to spend our money and they are given a blank check book with which to do it.

Another demographic challenge is that with the increase of retirees, more investment money will move away from the stock market and end up in less risky investment vehicles. Retirees will be looking for more secure, safer rates of return. This is a natural thought process, but it may have devastating results. In 3,000 days, for the first time in stock market history, more money may be moving out of 401(k) plans and the market in the form of retirement incomes, than new money going into such investments. It has been my observation that when more stocks are sold than bought, prices of those investments fall along with the values they hold in retirement programs. Can one-third of the working population in 3,000 days purchase the stocks being sold off by retirees and maintain share values even though there are less workers and less buyers to maintain company profits?

Unintended Consequences:
The Thought Process

In remarks at the 2002 National Summit on Retirement Savings, Alan Greenspan stated that because of the demographics of the country, it will be a real challenge to maintain the value of these retirement assets. He states, "This ever larger retired population will have to be fed, clothed, housed, and serviced by a work force growing far less rapidly. The retirees may have accumulated a large stock of retirement savings, but the goods and services needed to redeem those savings must be produced by an active work force assisted by a stock of plant and equipment sufficiently productive to meet the needs both of retirees and a work force expecting an ever increasing standard of living."[5] He goes on to say that ". . .the focus of the economy as a whole, of necessity, must be on producing the real resources needed to redeem the financial assets."[6]

In that same speech, Greenspan goes on to state that "[i]f the Social Security Trust Fund is depleted, the law requires that benefits are paid only to the extent that they can be financed out of current payroll tax receipts."[7] Do you really think a politician will allow this to happen? No, but it will take increased taxation and less benefits to keep them in existence.

---

[5]Speech on *Retirement Savings*, Alan Greenspan, February 28, 2002.

[6]*Id.*

[7]*Id.*

HANDWRITING ON THE WALL

The government knows it is between a rock and a hard place on the issue of Social Security. Greenspan's comments are an "I told you so" type of statement. "In addressing the impending retirement of those born just after WWII, we will need to consider whether Social Security should better align itself with the funding provisions of our private pension and annuity system. Policy makers need to consider these issues now if we are to ensure a comfortable retirement for the postwar generation, while at the same time according due consideration to the needs of the later generations that now make up our work force."[8]

The problem is the politicians spend our Social Security revenues faster than they are collected. If they would create a Social Security system with a public investment option, the government would lose control of that money. Remember, they consider it *their* money, not yours.

THEY DO IT WELL

In recent years, the government has become obsessed with imposing and collecting taxes. The collection of taxes has become job one and they do their job well. We are now being taxed at the highest levels in our history. Yet, even after collecting historical amounts of revenue in the form of taxes, the government continues to outspend these revenues and posts record amounts of debt. Even with all the proclaimed surpluses

---

[8] *Id.*

of the 90's, neither did taxes go down nor did government debt. In recent years, taxation has grown 42% faster than incomes.

One could argue that we have experienced tremendous growth in our standards of living. However, those increased standards have been fueled by a record amount of personal debt. Personal bankruptcies are at all time highs along with credit card debts. For the last several years, the average household has saved at a negative rate. Any sustained economic downturns or lethargic stock market results, or both, will do serious damage to future savings. Even though market losses can occur at any time, taxes will continue to increase. Why? Because they have to. The demographics of this country demand it.

IF WE KNOW SOMETHING FOR CERTAIN

Why did the government recently increase the levels that an individual can contribute to 401(k) plans and IRAs? Was this change initiated because they were concerned about your financial future OR THEIRS? They already know they are going to need larger pools of money to tax at whatever rate they can justify to finance the governments future liabilities. Read that again. They will tax retirement incomes at the highest rates achievable without jeopardizing their chances to get re-elected. A 401(k) or IRA simply defers taxation to a later date. It would be a different story if the government would guarantee that you would be taxed at the same tax level you were at when you put the money into these plans. Will they ever do that? No! They need and want as much of that money as they can get.

I can still hear the words echoing in the halls of

financial wisdom "You will probably retire to two-thirds of your income, and thus be in a lower tax bracket." Don't count on it! First of all, if you're working with a planner whose goal (because it's easy to achieve) is to retire you to two-thirds of your current income, do yourself a favor and <u>fire</u> him. They are telling you to retire with less money so you pay less taxes. Not a great solution. When you add the changing demographics, do you really think that, at any level, taxation is going to be lower in the future?

To get current levels of the public debt, go to: http://www.publicdebt.treas.gov/opd/opdpenny.htm. There, the current public debt of the government is listed daily. Look for the years in which large government surpluses were proclaimed and look for payments against this debt. Can you find any?

2002	$6,228,235,965,597.16
2001	$5,807,463,412,200.06
2000	$5,674,178,209,886.86
1999	$5,656,270,901,615.43
1998	$5,526,193,008,897.62
1997	$5,413,146,011,397.34
1996	$5,224,810,939,135.73
1995	$4,973,982,900,709.39
1994	$4,692,749,910,013.32
1993	$4,411,488,883,139.38
1992	$4,064,620,655,521.66
1991	$3,665,303,351,697.03
1990	$3,233,313,451,777.25
1989	$2,857,430,960,187.32[9]

---

[9]http://www.publicdebt.treas.gov

Now do you think that with this increasing debt to be paid, and the changing demographics of the country, that future taxation will be lower?

People should be hesitant to put money into government-sponsored retirement plans (401(k)s and IRAs) at a 28% tax bracket, knowing that upon retirement the tax levels could be, at that time, 35% or higher. Is that a 7% increase in taxes? No, that's almost a 30% increase in tax levels. Planners often recommend maximizing these plans without telling you about future demographics complications. The unintended consequences are lurking in the shadows. Why? Because some planner has determined that this information wasn't important for you to know. One thing you do need to know for certain, taxes will be waiting for you in the future. There will be fewer workers and more retirees and continued increases in government social programs and spending. That's for certain!

DOCTOR, IT HURTS WHEN I DO THIS

If it hurts you don't do it. The government's doctor says don't worry about the pain (paying unnecessary taxes) keep doing it until you die. Even then, taxes will be due but at least you won't feel the pain. Today, you need more knowledge so you are capable of making better financial decisions. The more you know the less pain you will suffer financially. The solutions to a rewarding financial future are not found just in the stock market. But that's what most people believe. Why? Because that's all they know. It is difficult to get the right solution when you start out with the wrong premise. Unless you work with someone who understands demographics and other wealth transfers and helps you eliminate or avoid them, your financial problems will continue and will compound and that is truly unfortunate.

REMEMBER WHO YOU ARE

Not only must you invest wisely but you must learn about the *Efficiency of Money* and wealth transfers. Your investments must be intertwined with these lessons to maximize your wealth no matter what level of wealth you are at. REMEMBER: The government sees you as a taxpayer. The bank sees you as a borrower. Investment companies see you as a fee payer. If you don't utilize the lessons of efficiency these organizations, the government, the banks, and investment companies will be first and foremost in your entire financial life. There will be no financial freedom until you can loosen the burdens in dealing with them.

THE LAST PICTURE SHOW

Imagine taking your spouse and kids to see a movie. You go into the theater, buy some popcorn and snacks. You find seats with no tall people in front of you and you start to relax. Looking around you notice an IRS agent that you're acquainted with. His family is with him. You continue looking around the theater and you notice your banker and his family are also there. A few rows behind them is your investment broker and her family. What a small world! The lights dim and the movie begins. About five minutes into the movie an usher comes down the main aisle and the lights come up. "Ladies and gentlemen we have a problem. There is a small fire in the lobby and we want everyone to leave calmly using the emergency exits." You're stunned. You look at your spouse and kids and say, "Don't worry, everything will be okay. Wait right here for one minute." You run over to the IRS agent and his family and help them out of the theater. Running back to your family you say "just one more minute", and you run back to help your banker and his family to the exits. This time on your way back you don't even stop at your family but simply give them that gesture with your index finger meaning you'll be right back. You continue running to assist your investment broker and her kids out of harms way. Finally, you get back to your family to secure their safety. They have that dumbfounded look on their faces and you realized you may have lost a few votes for the Parent of the Year Award.

FIRST, NOT LAST

This story may be irrational from a humane, loving standpoint. But from a financial standpoint, it is very true more times than not. The government, the banks, and investment companies have remedies to make sure that, in the event of something happening to you, they will still get paid....FIRST. Your family's outcome is of little consequence to them. Sustaining their financial future is more important to them than yours is. You must learn financial concepts and ideas that will put you and your family and your financial goals first. You must develop liquidity, use, and control of your money. You must also learn about lost opportunity cost. These concepts will increase your wisdom in making financial decisions. Knowing this, the next time your family is faced with a crisis or even new opportunities they will be <u>first</u>, not last.

ESTABLISHING YOUR BANKS

One of the goals is to help you see the transfers of wealth that you are involved in. These transfers could cost you hundreds of thousands of dollars. If you have the ability to save that money instead of giving it away, it would dramatically change your financial picture. In going through your finances, when we eliminate or reduce these transfers, you <u>will</u> save money. Since most of these transfers occur on a monthly basis, any money you save will be on an ongoing basis. The task of finding these transfers and reducing or eliminating them takes some time. Some changes may be necessary, but don't panic. You must stay committed to completing this task. Remember you will not spend one more dime than you are already spending.

Once we find your savings, I will refer to these savings as "banks." These "banks" are pools of money that you now own. When I refer to your "banks," I'm not talking about a physical, brick and mortar building. I'm talking about a pool of money that you will use strategically, for the rest of your life. It will not be uncommon to create two or three "banks" or pools of money for one person. Each "bank" that is created will have different characteristics. Some "banks" will be tax-free, some will be tax-sheltered. However, all of these "banks" will create liquidity, use, and control of your money. We want your "banks" to be very efficient.

USING IT

Knowing how to use your money is more important than what vehicle it's invested in. Many of today's assets are tied up in retirement plans and homes. Your "banks" will create sources of money to improve your lifestyle while reducing your wealth transfers. You will learn the value of establishing your personal "banks." You will then learn how to eliminate fees and interest you were paying to others. You will learn to reduce taxation and how to possibly lower some of your monthly payments. You will learn to turn bad debt (where the interest is not deductible) into good debt (where the interest is deductible). You will take these savings and bank them. You will learn how to make future purchases from your banks and pay <u>yourself</u> back, not others.

IDENTIFYING THE TRANSFERS OF YOUR WEALTH

To build the equity in your banks, we will be discussing the transfers of your wealth that occur everyday. Learning to identify your transfers is important. I will be discussing the most common transfers of wealth that many people face. When you recognize a transfer that you may be currently experiencing and how to reduce or eliminate it, you will be surprised. You will experience that defining moment in the way you think about money. Finding the transfers is only the first step. Building upon your savings is the second step, learning to utilize your savings is the third step, and replacing the savings after using them is the final lesson. By learning this cycle, you will create the velocity of money. This is a technique that banks, lending institutions, and credit card companies use everyday to transfer wealth from you to them. I personally have used my banks to purchase cars, take vacations, pay for education, help my children get a start in life, buy furniture, and make home improvements. I have always paid my banks back so the pool of money is always there when I need or want it.

GENERATIONAL BANKING

These techniques are not limited to just the parents of a family but also the grandparents. Gifts to minors has been a popular option for grandparents to give money to their children or grandchildren. Creating personal "banks" between the grandparents, children and grandchildren really opens up some financial doors that could prove to be very valuable. If the grandparents are financially secure, they too may discover a defining moment in their approach to money that they were going to leave to their families anyway upon death. You don't have to die to do this.

LOST OPPORTUNITY COST: THE FORGOTTEN FACTOR IN FINANCIAL CALCULATION

The definition of Lost Opportunity Cost (LOC) is this: If you spend a dollar, not only do you lose that dollar, but also the ability to earn money from that dollar. To give you an example of Lost Opportunity Cost (LOC), let's use the example of the cost of a wedding. The first lesson you must learn and remember is the mathematical Rule of 72. It works like this:

If you can get a 10% rate of return, your money will double every 7.2 years. If you get a 7.2% rate of return, your money will double every 10 years. This equation will come in very handy from here on out.

THE S&P 500

Back to the wedding. If you have ever planned one of these things, the first thing you must do is narrow it down to your closest 500 friends. I call them the special and privileged 500. Invitations, caterers, banquet halls, photographers, video photographers, entertainment, limos, wedding dresses, and fifty other things I can't remember push the cost close to the budget of a small city. Let's say the first down payment is $20,000. Let's also assume the bride and groom to be are 25 years old. If we use the Rule of 72 that $20,000 would double its value every 7.2 years if it earned a constant 10% rate of return. Watch how the values grow. . .

Age at 10% earning rate	Values	Age at 7.2% earning rate
25	$20,000	25
32.2	$40,000	35
39.4	$80,000	45
46.6	$160,000	55
53.8	$320,000	65
61	$640,000	75
68.2	$1,280,000	85

Now that you can see how the Rule of 72 works, let's take a look at Lost Opportunity Cost (LOC). If the $20,000 could have grown to $1,280,000, the LOC would be the difference between the $20,000 you spent and the $1,280,000 it could have become if you hadn't spent it. The future value of that $20,000 would have created substantial wealth if it had not been spent. The lost opportunity cost on the cost of the wedding is $1,260,000 (Lost Opportunity $1,280,000.00 minus Cost $20,000.00). Now that's a wedding!

Any purchases or transfers of your money via taxes, interest rates, fees, etc., create lost opportunity costs. Would it not be a wise decision to eliminate or reduce as many of these transfers as you can? In reducing these transfers you can truly watch your wealth grow. You can keep more of the money that you were unknowingly and unnecessarily giving away. Remember, in our example of the wedding couple, every dollar saved would grow to $64 by the time they were 68, assuming a 10% earnings rate.

This leads me to the next definition. The power of your money is useless unless you have liquidity, use, and control (LUC) of it. It's not where your money is deposited that is important, rather it's what you can do with it that is. There are so many vehicles that tie up our money: Mortgages, qualified plans, and instruments of debt. Whenever possible, you want your money to be liquid. *Liquidity* means being able to get your money <u>whenever</u> you want, without penalties or fees. *Use* of your money means being able to use your money any <u>way</u> you want. *Control* of your money means you don't have to go through a third party to get your money. I can best explain LUC by saying it will create options and opportunities for you, now and in the future. If an opportunity comes your way and you have no money to take advantage of it because all your money is tied up and not liquid, well, that is truly unfortunate. Do opportunities ever wait for you? Rarely. You must be financially ready. If you're not you're at the mercy of lending institutions.

NOW THAT'S AN <u>UGLY</u> BABY!

In order to make solid financial decisions, it is important to be able to recognize the difference between opinions and facts. If you have ever been to a maternity ward and viewed the newborn babies, I bet you can pick out one that in a cute way, is sort of ugly. The thing is, you will never be able to convince the mother that her child is ugly. You see, one's opinion can sometimes outweigh the facts. If we have done a chore the same way our entire lives, we believe that our way is the <u>only</u> way to do that chore. Does being comfortable with things we do make it a <u>fact</u> that it is the best way to do it? No, over a period of time we simply create an inability to change. To give you an example, I believe my father had four kids just to change stations on the TV for him. I know he was the last person in the U. S. to buy a remote control for his TV. Even then, my mother believed that if not properly aimed, you could break things or knock pictures off the wall with the remote. I even caught my dad aiming it at my mother once.

The fact is that people don't know the facts. In finances, some may believe that stuffing the mattresses full with money is the best way to save. To them, it's the only way they know to save, so it becomes a fact. I think their savings could go up in smoke, but that's only my opinion.

GIVE ME A SHOVEL

As a society, we are given so much information it is almost impossible to decipher between opinion and fact. There is an enormous amount of misinformation that has been passed on, passed down, or advertised that is not fully the truth or fact. We receive bits and pieces upon which our decisions are based. When it comes to finances, misinformation or half truths may lead us down a path toward unintended consequences. You must learn to dig A LAYER DEEPER. Every one of your financial decisions creates opportunities either for you or others. Unfortunately, its usually the latter. The process of learning to think A LAYER DEEPER will create more wealth for you by reducing the money you transfer to third parties. In thinking a LAYER DEEPER, you will use your newfound tools of knowledge, the Rule of 72, LUC and LOC to uncover the information you need to make better financial decisions. How will these decisions play out when it comes to the demographics of the country? Is this the right decision for you? (YOU ARE NOW STARTING TO THINK FOR YOURSELF, INSTEAD OF BEING TOLD WHAT TO THINK). It's not difficult. What is difficult is being able to decipher opinion from fact, myth from reality, without the proper use of common sense and knowledge. The lack of knowledge is your largest wealth transfer.

SHE ONLY DROVE IT TO CHURCH ON SUNDAYS

More often than not we make decisions based on what we know, whether we know a lot or very little. We rely on the information that is given to us by others to help us make these decisions. Many times, when something is sold we are told the positive aspects of the sale item. The seller stands to profit and, unfortunately, any negative aspects of the sale will be underplayed. The seller's intent maybe honorable but you must understand how to decipher what isn't said. That comes with knowledge. You see, many people have thoughts but don't know how to think. What effect would it have on a buyer if the used car salesperson said, "She only drove the car to church on Sundays," only to find out later that after church, she had to have the car towed back to her house every week? Without all the information, the sales person deprived you the opportunity to make well thought-out financial decisions.

YOUR NEED TO KNOW:
CONFUSION BETWEEN OPINION AND FACT

As I said before, some people have thoughts, but don't know how to think. It's hard to get the right solution when you start out with the wrong premise. We have been told very little when it comes to transferring our wealth away unknowingly and unnecessarily. The government professes to have your best interest at heart. If they did, don't you think they would sponsor infomercials every week on how to greatly reduce your taxes? I'm sure they could do that if they wanted to. But why should they? They are in the business of collecting taxes. Do they have your best interests in mind? Does the 47,000 pages of tax code affect your need to know? Do banks sponsor infomercials about reducing the interest that they charge you? NO. Does your accountant spend hours and hours with you teaching you how to be efficient with your money? NO. Why won't these groups help you do this? Because there is no money in it for them and it would affect the amount of money they can collect from you. Do you think they want to control YOUR NEED TO KNOW so they can increase their profits on tax revenues? YES! Do these people give us financial advice? YES! Does something smell funny here? Think about it. Do you think the government, banks, and accounting firms are interested in financing your future or theirs? There could be a conflict of interest here.

A REAL WORK OF ART

Picture a little Mexican boy dressed in a sombrero and poncho, tattered and worn. He is sitting on a log, shoeless, dirty, with a somber look on his face. Our first impression might be poverty in Mexico. Now if were able to enlarge the picture around this little boy, you would find out that he is a little boy playing with his friends in Central Park. Often we are given only a glimpse of the financial picture we should see. If given the opportunity to see the whole picture, we might come up with different financial conclusions. Unfortunately, others are determining what you should see. Not being able to see whole pictures may cause unintended consequences for you in the future.

DUMB AND DUMBER

Every step of our education has been centered on <u>what</u> to think, rather than <u>how</u> to think. We have been dumbed-down as a society. When it comes to finances, the less we know, the more we are exposed to misinformation. All the financial information that is available to us today has created some wealth, but has also created a debt-ridden society with record numbers of bankruptcies. Where are the financial lessons and who is teaching them? Are we getting the whole story? The solution is the understanding that knowledge is power and you must learn concepts that put you in control of your financial future.

CRYSTAL BALL FOR SALE

I'm going to step out on a ledge here. I really don't believe in the way financial planning is being sold to the American public. That's not to say I don't believe in financial planning, I just don't believe in the way it is being packaged, marketed, and sold. There are some great people in the industry that do tremendous, honest work. There are also many who call themselves financial planners who are about as smart as a bag full of hammers. In a world full of "wanna-bes," the title *financial planner* has been bounced around more than a beach ball at a rock concert. Their solution to your financial future is based on the sales goals of their companies. Their assumptions and recommendations are less accurate than a six year old predicting the weather. Yet they produce 15 pages of numbers, charts, and graphs in multiple colors that looks as if they are really serious about what they do. The problem is, by the time the ink is dry and reviewed by the victim, I mean client, the numbers are wrong. The second problem is that there is no <u>knowledge</u> in that report, just assumptions and guesses at future results. If someone broke the crystal ball we would have to rely on knowledge and there is very little of that floating around. Understanding the future demographics we must face, knowledge about liquidity, use, and control of your money, lost opportunity costs, why you aren't being told what you need to know, and the difference between opinion and fact will shape a new foundation in the way you think about finances. None of these lessons will be found on a page full of numbers and graphs. Just as buying a couple of investments from a financial planner doesn't solve all of your financial problems.

WHO'S THE BOSS HERE?

I learned a long time ago that the situation you confront is always the boss. You face different challenges everyday, but in most cases you have the knowledge and flexibility to conquer them. Without knowledge and flexibility, your problems will control you and you will no longer be the boss of those challenges. This is true of your finances also. You need knowledge that will create options, in order to stay in control of the never ending changes in your financial landscape.

IT'S NOT AS HARD AS IT LOOKS

Many times planners make things much more complicated than they need to be. The first step in getting a grasp on your finances is to understand there are only three types of money - Lifestyle money, accumulated money, and transferred money.

LIFESTYLE MONEY

Lifestyle money is the amount of money needed to maintain your standard of living. The house you live in, the cars, vacations, the country club, all the comforts your accustomed to. You work really hard and deserve some affordable quality of life. You are very aware of this type of money because you live with it everyday. All of your financial decisions are based around your lifestyle or standard of living. Everyone I know would like to improve their lifestyle for themselves and their families. If you live above these standards, you run the risk of overbearing debt and some future unintended consequences with your accumulated money.

ACCUMULATED MONEY

Accumulated money is money you save in vehicles such as savings programs, retirement plans, and bank savings. It is here, in accumulated money, where almost everyone's attention is focused. Banks, financial planners, investment brokers, financial magazines, news articles, and anyone who considers themselves a financial wizard are active in this area. Confusion reigns supreme here. Trying to separate the opinions from fact, the myth from reality, and the truth from fiction is an impossibility. Misinformation and slight of hand are used as tools of the trade and sound bits make good headlines. Greed and ambition motivate individuals and corporations to forego the truth whenever it is convenient and profitable. Enron, Arthur Anderson, WorldCom, and Kmart are just a few examples of the lengths some will go to succeed, at the price of others.

Yogi Berra said it: The future isn't what it used to be. He's right. In your accumulated money, it is important to get good, sound financial help. Having someone who understands the transfers of your wealth, demographics, LUC, and LOC is a must. They will be skilled in the area reducing or eliminating transfers of your wealth you make everyday, unknowingly and unnecessarily.

TRANSFERRED MONEY

The third type of money is transferred money. We transfer most of our wealth away every day, unknowingly and unnecessarily. Transfers appear in the form of taxes, interest rates, fees, finance charges, maintenance fees, management fees, etc., etc. The recipients of these transfers are the Federal, State, and local governments, banks, loan companies, mortgage companies, and investment companies. We will be discussing some of these in detail, but for now understand that transfers consume a lot of your money. Understanding this third type of money is the secret. While everyone is focusing on accumulated money, the answers to increasing your wealth lay hidden in your transfers. Here you can create more wealth without spending a single additional dime or facing any market risks. We can recapture some of that transferred money, and use it to finance your future and increase your standard of living.

THREE TYPES

All of the money you have ends up in one of the aforementioned three types: Lifestyle, accumulated, or transferred. A common goal of almost everyone is to have their wealth grow. Unfortunately, when we increase our incomes, improve our standard of living, and save more money for the future, we also trigger some unintended consequences. As we experience growth, we also increase taxation and the possibility of greater taxation down the road. Even increasing our savings for retirement will create greater amounts of taxation. It seems every time we try to save a dollar we will have to give another dollar away.

While expanding our standard of living, we purchase new homes, cars, TVS, and furniture mostly on credit, which creates greater amounts of debt and higher interest payments transferred to others. Let's face it, almost all our purchases are depreciating assets. When you drive the new car off the showroom floor its value drops 30% and continues to drop in value year after year. Your new home may increase in value, but it is surrounded by transfers in the form of interest rates, property tax, school tax, water and sewer tax, maintenance, and comfort improvements.

Banks and credit companies look at this as, "a dollar for you, a dollar for me" opportunity. Unfortunately, with the exception of mortgage interest, debt interest is not tax deductible. If you had the opportunity to recapture some of these dollars your transferring to others would you do it? Absolutely! But most people don't know how. No one is teaching you how to do it, with reason. If a bank taught you how to reduce interest payments, they would be lowering their profit levels, so they are not going to do it.

The problem of increasing your standard of living creates the unintended consequence of increasing your money transfers. Some people would look at the problem of debt by simply paying cash for something, thinking they will eliminate interest transfers to the bank. Here lies another hidden problem. If you're 40 years old and pay $5,000.00 cash for something, not only do you lose the $5,000.00, but also the ability to earn money from that $5,000.00. A lost opportunity cost. At a 7% earning rate, the value of that $5,000.00 is $20,000.00 in 20 years. You must learn the difference, the value to you, whether you use your money for a purchase or someone else's (the banks). You must learn how to make these decisions. When you do, your wealth will grow. Now, if the interest paid on your debt was deductible from your taxes, it might change your thought process about paying cash for an item.

CONGRATULATIONS, YOU'VE BECOME
A MORE PERFECT TAXPAYER

Remember who created these programs, the government and banks. They stand to profit the most if you involve yourself in their traps, I mean plans. Transfers, transfers, transfers, will kill financial growth.

GUARANTEED

Compliance officers get really nervous when they see this word. When investing in stocks and mutual funds this word, the "G" word, disappears. In discussing transfers, I am allowed to use this word in the following example.

If someone is earning $75,000.00 in income per year and is saving $5,000.00, they would have $70,000.00 of residual income. This $70,000.00 is spent on mortgage payments, car payments, clothes, food, taxes, etc., to sustain their standard of living. Like most average families, at the end of the year, the $70,000.00 has been spent. If I showed them how to save just 1% of that $70,000.00, it would create $700.00 in savings. That savings represents a 14% increase on the $5,000.00 they were saving. That's right, a 14% increase, guaranteed, with no market risk. Most people, when they learn how to do this, save a lot more than 1%. When applied properly, savings of 5% to 7% are achievable from your transferred money.

FOCUSING ON 4%

Unfortunately most planners focus in on the 3% or 4% of money people think they can save from their lifestyle money. Most planners will advise you to try to save even more money than that, reducing your standard of living money to grow your accumulated money. When more money flows out of your lifestyle money, your standard of living is decreased. Do you think it would be important to find the money for savings from other than your lifestyle? If you continue to divert money only from your lifestyle, pretty soon you can't afford to go on vacation, buy a new car, or make home improvements.

YOUR DOLLAR

To examine how your money is affected by transfers, you really have to think many layers deeper. First, you have to obtain for a job or career. Your services or labor has value to the employer and you will be compensated for it. The employer already knows what they can afford to pay you. Their determination of your pay comes from many different equations, most of which are transfers of company profits that ultimately affect your pay scale. Company profits determine whether or not they can afford to pay you. The level of company profits are determined after all expenses have been paid. Expenses include not only everyday business activities, but also corporate taxes, payroll taxes, government regulations and fees (taxes), property taxes, unemployment taxes, workman's comp taxes, possible sales tax, operating licenses, utilities that include taxes (passed on to the consumer), water, gas, electric, city and state tax. Of course this company, like all others, will pass off the cost of its taxation by raising the price of anything they sell to you and me, the consumer.

SO YOU GOT THE JOB. . . LET'S PARTY!

After they have tapped the corporation for taxes, the government moves on to much easier prey: You. You decide to throw a party upon receiving your first paycheck. The government shows up, and it congratulates you on your new position by taking about 30% of your pay. That's just the Feds. The state also crashes the party, and takes its cut of your money, along with the city in which you live. A few more show up for your first check-cashing party. The county people are there with their hands out for county taxes. The entire school board shows up in their limos looking for their share. They are the ones looking underneath your couch cushions for loose change. The water and sewer guys show up too. Good thing only one of them came in while the other five wait out in the truck for a couple of hours. The gas and electric people are also there, saying their fees and taxes are included in the monthly statement. You look around and think, "I better go cash this check so I can afford all of this." You go to the bank and, yep, there's a check cashing fee, even though you have your mortgage with them and $200.00 in their savings account paying you a whopping 1½%. By the way, the government makes you pay a tax on the money you make on that too.

You know the company that hired you has passed on its cost and taxes on to you, the employee, indirectly, by paying you less. The balance is passed on to the consumers. The federal, state, county, and city governments pass on the expenses to you as a taxpayer. The utility companies do the same thing and they include their fees and taxes billed directly to you. The school board (property taxes), pass everything they do, and I mean everything, onto the consumer. The party is over!!!

IMPORTANT QUESTIONS

Who do you pass <u>your</u> expenses on to? What relief do <u>you</u> have to recapture these dollars? None? Would you agree these transfers are killing you financially? Do you feel hundreds of people are profiting from you with no relief in site? If you could learn to reduce these transfers and keep the money, your money, for yourself, would you do it?

You take what little is left of your money and make your car payment. The payment includes interest to the lender. Simply driving the car creates other transfers. Gas prices which include several taxes. A fee (tax) to renew your driver's license, license plate fees (tax) due every year, insurance premiums in which the insurance companies fees and taxes are passed on to you and any maintenance needed, parts and labor which is also taxed. Also, the value of this car does decrease every year. You finally figure out the only way you can pass on your expenses to someone else and pay for all of this is to ask for a raise from your employer. This solution may also have unintended consequences. The employer may decide they can't afford you and lets you go. Or you get a raise only to find out it increases the amount of taxes you pay. Study the transfers of your wealth that you are making, obtain the knowledge, make changes, and reduce the transfers.

HIDDEN TRANSFERS

Not only is just about everything you buy a depreciating asset, it will probably have to be replaced in the future. Another form of tax on your wealth is inflation. When you replace these goods in the future, they will most likely cost more. Personal and corporate taxes and government regulations have more to do with prices going up than the old standard: "corporate greed." In the same breath, corporations will do just about anything to show profits to their shareholders. Once again, the added factor of the changing demographics of our nation will also complicate the challenge of you trying to hang on to your money. Finally, no amount of planning will ever prevent dumb luck.

IF I COULD TELL YOU THE <u>EXACT</u> DAY THAT YOUR RETIREMENT ACCOUNT WOULD SUFFER ITS GREATEST LOSSES, WOULD YOU WANT TO KNOW THAT DAY?

THEN IN KNOWING THAT DAY, IF YOU COULD DO SOMETHING NOW TO PREVENT THOSE LOSSES, WOULD YOU DO IT?

MAJOR TRANSFERS OF YOUR WEALTH

In your everyday existence, you are confronted with transfers of your wealth. You continuously, unknowingly and unnecessarily, give or transfer money away. Not only do you give this money away but you also lose the ability to earn money on that money once it is transferred. This compounds your loss. To eliminate or reduce these transfers ,you must first learn to recognize them and then understand how directly or indirectly they cost you money. You may have to confront conventional financial wisdom. Remember, the ones giving you these financial programs tend to profit from them. Always ask, who would profit from these transfers? Here is a list of the transfers of your wealth we will be discussing:

- Taxes
- Qualified Retirement Plans
- Financial Planning
- Disability
- Credit cards

- Tax refunds
- Owning a home
- Life Insurance
- Purchasing Cars
- Investments

These ten transfers can create financial losses for you. You must study each one and determine how they will affect you. On the surface, the transfers seem pretty basic. It is not until you think a layer deeper that you find that these transfers may cause unintended consequences in the future. The future demographics of the country will affect everyone's financial future.

THE TRANSFERS

TRANSFER 1:

TAXES

THE LARGEST TRANSFER
OF YOUR WEALTH...
ARE YOU FINANCING YOUR FUTURE,
OR THE GOVERNMENT'S?

A common definition of the word "tax" might be: "A contribution for the support of a government required of persons, groups, or businesses within the domain of that government." "A burdensome or excessive demand, a strain." The only power an elected official has is his ability to spend money, our money. The one thing the government does well is collect taxes. The problem is they spend more than they collect. The government now spends a majority of its time trying to raise revenue through taxes in order to continue their increased spending. Forty percent of your income now goes to some form of tax, which is more than the average family spends on food, clothing and housing. According to the Family Research Council in 1996, since 1948 for a family of four with an average income, Federal tax rates are up 1,250%.[10] Over the past 10 years, state and local government taxes have increased 168% faster than national incomes.[11] Overall, we are now being taxed at a higher rate than when we threw tea into the

---

[10]Michael Hodges, *Tax Report - A chapter of the Grandfather Economic Reports*, April, 2002, *at* <http://mwhodges.home.att.net/tax.htm>.

[11]*Id.*

harbor, with no end of increases in sight. Now include the understanding of the demographics of our nation, and that light at the end of the tunnel is not a ray of sunshine, but a train coming our way and we're on the tracks.

Income taxes have been the central focus of many debates. Most financial planners mention only a couple of taxes that may affect a client's future. These are usually the income tax and the estate tax. These two taxes are formidable foes of wealth, yet they represent only the tip of the iceberg when it comes to the overall taxation that really exists. Here is a list of taxes that you are confronted with on a daily basis:

FEDERAL INCOME TAX
SOCIAL SECURITY TAX
STATE TAX
CITY TAX
COUNTY TAX
PROPERTY TAX
PERSONAL PROPERTY TAX
SCHOOL TAX
LONG CAPITAL GAINS TAX
SHORT CAPITAL GAINS TAX
SALES TAX
ESTATE TAX
GASOLINE TAX
WATER TAX
SEWER TAX
TAX ON ENERGY – GAS
                    ELECTRIC
                    HEATING OIL
BUSINESS TAX
AIRPORT TAX
TELEPHONE TAX

**LICENSE PLATE TAX
HOTEL TAX
CABLE TV TAX
USER TAXES
UNEMPLOYMENT TAX
WORKERS COMP. TAX
100'S OF REGULATORY FEES**

It is probably safe to say that if something is not taxed it must be illegal. Drugs, prostitution, theft, money laundering, etc. would be at the top of the non-taxed industries. After examining this list of taxes one could come to the conclusion that taxes, now and in the future, represent the largest transfer you will face in your life and possibly after your death. If instead of taking taxes out of our paychecks and taxing us for our purchases, they sent everyone a tax bill at the end of each month for us to pay, there would be a revolution!

NO ONE TOLD ME

If it came to your attention that you were unknowingly and unnecessarily paying a tax you didn't have to, would you continue to pay it? If you were told to pay a certain amount of tax, would you purposely over pay that amount due? If you could legally recapture or keep some of the money you pay in taxes, would you do it? If no one has taught you techniques of reducing taxation when you can, that is truly unfortunate. The most common belief is that using qualified plans is the best way to reduce taxation. This is what you are told to believe. Don't be surprised to find out that this is not necessarily true. The tax savings we're talking about here is not about loading up your IRA or 401(k) plans. Once again it may be quite the opposite.

ITS ONLY TEMPORARY

In 1913, the 16th Amendment of the U. S. Constitution was passed, allowing the federal government to impose an income tax on the citizens of the United States.[12] Ironically, 20 years prior to that, as part of a trade bill, the government passed into law an income tax that the Supreme Court struck down as unconstitutional. But persistence paid off, and Congress ratified the 16th amendment in October, 1913.[13] The tax measure was passed as a temporary measure. The original federal marginal tax was around 6%, and initially only about 5% of the population had to file tax statements.[14]

Clearly, the federal government wasn't shy about raising income taxes. During World War I and World War II, the marginal tax rates were high and remain at a level of over 50% for almost 50 years.

---

[12]Grandfather article

[13]The Century Foundation. Tax Reform. New York: The Century Foundation Press, 1999.

[14]Id.

UNDERSTANDING THE MATH

Recently, I happened to come across my father's 1960 tax return. The federal marginal tax rate that year was 87%. I thought, how did my parents ever survive with four kids and a dog? My father worked two jobs and we survived without having to eat the dog. Back then he was told the same story that we sometimes hear today about retirement income: That he would probably retire to two-thirds of his income, thus be in a lower tax bracket. In 1960, although the marginal tax rate was 87%, just about everything my father purchased was deductible on his tax return. After his deductions, his realized tax bracket was around 12%. Well my father did retire to two-thirds of his income, but retired to a 28% tax bracket. Now, you might say that the difference between a 12% tax bracket and a 28% tax bracket is just 16%. Not quite. It was an increase of almost 140% in his taxation level. Soon after retirement the dog disappeared.

In the tax reform acts of the 1980's, the government professed to give its citizens one of the lowest federal tax brackets in the history of the country. Numerically they did, but they quietly took away most of the deductions. It created one of the largest windfalls in the government's taxation history. It was amazing. . . politicians proclaimed lower taxes while we actually paid more. The next leader came in and said "Read my lips, no new taxes." The next thing you know the federal marginal tax rate went from 31% to 39%. Check your math. Is that an eight percent increase? NO! It's about a 27% increase in taxation. Remember, all those increases were put in place with no tax deductions. A double whammy. Once again, even with the record tax revenues being collected, the country's debt continues to grow. In the near future, the demographics of the country will compound the taxation issues causing major problems. Does anyone really believe taxes will go down in the future? If your income is so small when you retire that your taxes actually go down, I feel sorry for you. Get help.

No matter how you look at it, taxes will continue to be the largest transfer of your wealth now and in the future. If you believe what the government tells you about its retirement plans and deferring taxation to a later date, I would encourage you once again to study the demographics of the country. I believe the government's main objective is to thrive and survive. Meanwhile, on the streets of America, we the public struggle to do the same thing. Remember, you and I the taxpayers, are the only ones paying for this. There is no such thing as a free lunch. Every time you earn a dollar, spend a dollar, and save a dollar, you face possible taxation. Any attempt by you to thrive or survive will be taxed. The real unfortunate fact is, they can change the tax rules anytime it suits or profits them. Trying to plan your financial future without understanding the inevitable changes the government must make, is like building a home on quicksand. Is the government's goal to finance their future or yours? Their plans may also create unintended consequences for you.

SIT DOGGY SIT

Around and around he went as fast as he could with the never ending quest of catching his tail. At first, watching a dog chase his tail is sort of funny. As the dog persists and starts panting it becomes less humorous. Pretty soon you feel sorry for the animal and try to stop him. "Sit doggy sit." He stops for a second then starts all over again, chasing his tail. You think to yourself what would he do if he caught it? What's the point? First of all, this dog needs help, but to him it's a normal way of life. To me, the dog catching his tail is like someone trying to get a tax refund. You go round and round, get dizzy, work really hard pursuing it, spent a lot of time and effort to get it, only to find out it was yours in the first place.

TRANSFER 2:

TAX REFUNDS
AVOIDING TAX EXUBERANCE

The concept of overpaying for something really makes my blood boil. Have you ever been on an airplane and overheard the couple next to you say they spent $200 less than you did for your ticket on CheapTickets.com. First you're mad, then you feel stupid. You would have to be tortured to admit you overpaid.

I can never understand the exuberance people feel when they get a tax refund. They worked all year and paid taxes then went round and round, got dizzy, worked hard to get it back, spent a lot of time doing it, only to find out it was theirs all along. They act as if they won something when in all actuality, they lost.

What is the rate of return the government gives you on overpayment of taxes, otherwise known as a refund? Zero percent. In some cases, you have to hire an accountant to help you get this overpayment back. Since they used your money all year long, did you even get a thank you letter? Let me get this straight. You gave them too much money. They gave you a zero percent rate of return. You had to pay an accountant to help you get it back and they didn't say thanks. You will have to torture me to admit that I received a tax refund.

The average refund is almost enough to make a car payment every month for the whole year. A $3,000 refund would create $250 a month to improve your standard of living. You would also have the opportunity to invest it and earn even more money. The most important result of adjusting your withholding on your paycheck is that you would have liquidity, use, and control of your money that you normally would have overpaid to the government. I would rather owe the government $100 on April 15th than have them owe me something.

Say you went to a clothing store and found a jacket that you liked. You walked to the cashier to pay for the $110.00 garment, hand her $200.00 and she rings it up. She comes back and says, "Thank you. Your change will be mailed to you in about a year." You in turn say, "That will be fine." Yeah right! But isn't that the way the government deals with us? Make sure your withholdings are adjusted properly so you won't suffer from tax exuberance.

THE PROBLEM IS THE SOLUTION
AND THE SOLUTION IS THE PROBLEM

The government SEEMS to have gone out of its way to help you save money and taxes. The important word there is "seems." They have created savings programs with the idea you will save taxes by participating in them. Why? Possibly out of guilt for having overtaxed you in the first place. Possibly because high current taxation has forced us, as a country, to save at a <u>negative</u> rate. Possibly the governments own fear that social security and other social programs will be forced to change dramatically. Possibly because the government understands the demographics of the changing population and the effects it will have on social programs. Possibly to shift the blame for less retirement income from them to you. Possibly because introducing these programs may help them get re-elected. Maybe, just maybe, they are interested in financing their future not yours. Everyone will agree that tax deferred savings is a good idea. But the government will decide what rate of taxation will be assessed when you take withdrawals. Wouldn't it be a coincidence if the government were able to collect more tax revenues from you by using these programs? If they were truly that concerned about our savings, wouldn't they simply lower taxes? If they were that concerned, why do they even tax what little we are able to save?

WHO PAYS?

There are many types of government-sponsored savings plans. They allow you to save money, if you qualify, in tax-deferred programs. Some of these plans such as defined benefit, defined contribution, and profit sharing plans to name a few, require the employer to make contributions to these plans on your behalf. The plans are disappearing more and more because it is becoming very costly for companies to maintain them. This first group of plans, although laden with regulation, are a great benefit to the employee. None of the workers' money goes directly into these plans. These plans are funded by the employer.

The second type of plan enables the employer and the employee both to contribute to the plan with restrictions of course. The employer will match a certain dollar amount or percentage of the employee contribution. Matching contributions by the employer is an option. It is not uncommon for the employer not to contribute anything. One of the most familiar plans that fall into this category is the 401(k). The 401(k) made it easier and less expensive than the old traditional retirement plans for the employer. Why? For the cost of administering the plan, a company can proclaim that it offers benefits for its employees. Even though the employee is funding most, if not all, of the plan.

The third type of plan that was created is one where the participant funds the entire program. IRAs, 401(k)s, and others are the most widely used plans by most individuals. Since these are the most commonly used I am going to focus on these plans.

When it comes to transfers of your wealth I wanted to simplistically separate these plans by one factor: Who pays for these programs. If you can get someone to help fund your retirement with money, terrific, do it! But as for the money you contribute into these plans <u>without</u> company matches, I want you to start thinking a layer deeper. If you're funding the full amount for these plans, there are things you need to know in considering whether or not to participate in them.

My intent here was not to explain and describe how these plans work and all their complexities, but simply to examine where is the funding coming from, and to discover who is encouraging the use these plans and why.

MAGICIAN'S ASSISTANT

Step right up, come one come all, to the greatest disappearing act ever performed. Watch in amazement as the master of deception makes things disappear with the help of his assistants. Watch as entire fortunes vanish into thin air. Your participation is mandatory and our assistants will prepare you for the show. Welcome to the greatest show on earth.

The government creates the plans, and financial professionals deliver them. With little or no questioning, it is believed that life can not exist without government savings plans. They are marketed by banks, accountants, brokers, insurance and investment companies. All of these companies promote these savings programs because they profit from their existence. It would also be logical that the ones who created them would also profit. The popularity of these plans are based on blind faith. It is assumed, if the government and all these professionals support these programs, they must be good. Even companies offer these programs as a benefit to its employees. All of these seem to be tremendous tools for saving for retirement. When you get to retirement, HOCUS POCUS, POOF! A whole lot of your money disappears. Along with it, so does the magician and the assistants.

WHOSE FUTURE ARE YOU FINANCING . . .

YOURS, OR THE GOVERNMENT'S?

TRANSFER 3:

<u>QUALIFIED</u>
<u>RETIREMENT PLANS</u>
THINKING A LAYER DEEPER

I, for one, don't believe qualified retirement plans are all that they profess to be. They are surrounded by ever-changing, complicated rules that can turn out to be very costly. I do believe qualified plans serve a purpose. At best, I believe they force people to save, which is something that people could do on their own with little discipline. I don't believe all the rhetoric about tax savings. Someone is going to be taxed on this money. If not you, then your heirs. The question is, at what rate will it be taxed?

TAX SAVINGS: REAL OR APPARENT?

I want to share with you an example of a 45 year-old person who was told they should have an IRA so they could generate tax savings. I gave this example to a group of accountants. I told them I would give $100.00 to each accountant who came up with the right answer. The question was this: If a 45 year old person, in a 28% tax bracket that qualified for an IRA put $2,000 into an IRA, what would the tax savings be for that person? [I know the amount that can be deposited into IRAs has changed, just bear with me for the sake of the example.] I told them to write the answer on the back of their business card and pass them forward. Everyone of them passed their card forward positive that they would be $100.00

richer. I reviewed all the cards. They all said the same thing, $560.00. Which they figured by taking 28% of $2,000.00. I hesitated and then asked, "Is this tax savings real or apparent?"

I went to the chalk board, and wrote these numbers:

Age	IRA plan growing at 10%
45	$2,000
52	$4,000
59	$8,000
66	$16,000

By simply using the Rule of 72, at 10% rate of return the money would double about every seven years. All the CPAs agreed with this calculation. I then told them every card they sent forward on it had the answer as $560.00. None of them seemed surprised. I then asked them, if this person could invest the $560.00 tax savings, what would that look like assuming I could get a 10% rate of return on that money?

Age	Tax savings growth at 10%
45	$560
52	$1,120
59	$2,240
66	$4,480

Saving $16,000.00 in an IRA, investing the purported tax savings and having those savings grow to $4,480.00 looked great. I then combined the two charts:

Age	IRA savings at 10%	Tax savings at 10%
45	$2,000	$560
52	$4,000	$1,120
59	$8,000	$2,240
66	$16,000	$4,480

Now this person turns 66 years old and wishes to withdraw $16,000.00, along with other savings. Miraculously, they are still in a 28% tax bracket at the time of withdrawal. His accountant reminds him that he has to pay taxes on it at withdrawal.

Interestingly, the tax due on that $16,000.00 withdrawn is $4,480.00. Exactly what we thought was saved in the tax savings account. Where is the tax savings? To make matters worse, there is another problem: Capital gains on the tax savings account. Over the 21 years of saving in my example, $784.00 had to be paid in capital gains taxes. This lowers the tax savings account to $3,696.00. Now this person had a tax due of $4,480.00 and had only $3,696.00 to pay the tax. Where is the tax savings?

WE'RE NOT DONE YET

If you understand the demographics of the country, you will come to the conclusion that you will very likely retire to a higher tax bracket. Look what happens to the apparent savings now:

Age	IRA savings at 10%	Tax savings at 10%
45	$2,000	$560
52	$4,000	$1,120
59	$8,000	$2,240
66	$16,000	$4,480
	Capital Gains Tax	-$784
	Savings after tax	$3,696

Tax due at withdrawal:
  28% tax bracket= $4,480
  35% tax bracket= $5,600
  40% tax bracket= $6,400

Hocus Pocus, Poof! The tax savings disappears! Once again I asked the accountants, "Where is the tax savings?" I then calmly put the $100.00 back into my pocket. No one argued my calculation. No one argued the results or even the demographics. Most agreed it will be problem in the future.

After my example, I spoke to some of the accountants and I asked if they would still recommend IRAs to some of their clients. Some said yes. They said it is their job to get clients <u>refunds,</u> which implies tax savings. "Regardless of the consequences?" I asked. "Yes," was the reply. Interpretation: It was not necessary that their clients know the facts about IRAs. It is possible that the decisions of these accountants could cause larger transfers of their clients' wealth in the future, unknowingly and unnecessarily.

TAX A DERBY

If I can tell you the exact day that your qualified retirement account will suffer its greatest loss, would you want to know that day? And in knowing that day, if we could do something now to prevent these losses, would you do it?

Taxes are the largest transfers of your wealth. The day you activate your qualified retirement account is the day that it will suffer its greatest loss, due to <u>taxation</u>, not because of losses in the stock market. 100% of your qualified retirement income becomes taxable. Congratulations, you've become the perfect taxpayer.

WHAT WE HAVE HERE IS A FAILURE TO COMMUNICATE

You may consider other complications that surround qualified plans. Many people suffer from a lack of liquidity, use, and control of their money. Qualified plans limit the amount of access you have to your money. If this is the only source of your savings you may consider diversifying into more non-qualified accounts also. Limiting your access to your money may also limit your options and opportunities in the future.

If you ask what would happen if you were to take money out of your IRA before the age of 59 ½ , what would the typical response be? You will be taxed on the amount you took out and penalized 10% of that amount for early withdrawal. Tax professionals consider this a major no-no. They will tell you if you wanted to withdraw $1,000.00 and you were in a 28% tax bracket that you would lose $280.00 in taxes and penalized $100.00 to boot. They will give you that "What are you, stupid?" look and tell you your going to lose $380.00.

Let's get one thing straight. You were going to get taxed on this money either now or later. The thought that you will lose money for early withdrawal by being taxed for it is misleading, since it will be taxed no matter what. Perhaps if you study the demographics of the country, once again you may come to the conclusion that there is a possibility you will be taxed on that money at a higher rate. The 10% penalty on the early withdrawal is a reality, unless . . .

HAVE YOU HEARD THIS ONE

Accessing IRA funds before the age of 59½ without incurring the 10% penalty is permissible under the IRS notice 89-25-IRB 1989-12.68 section 72t by using one of the three following distribution methods: 1) Life expectancy; 2) Amortization; and 3) Annuitization. The life expectancy method simply calculates the amount which can be withdrawn annually, by dividing your account balance by your life expectancy based on tables furnished by the IRS. The second method is amortization, which allows you to amortize your account balance based on a projection of what your account might earn over your lifetime. The IRS requires that the interest rate assumed in this calculation be "reasonable." For the annuitization method, the IRS also allows withdrawal based on a life insurance mortality table (UP-1984) and a "reasonable" interest rate assumption. This method normally generates the largest withdrawal.

Now why any financial professional would withhold this information from you is beyond me. But it is obvious that someone has decided that you didn't need to know this. If something you thought to be true wasn't true, when would you want to know about it? It is possible to avoid the 10% penalty for early withdrawals from an IRA.

In the event you have a 401(k) and lose your job or retire early, transferring your 401(k) to an IRA will allow 72t distributions. 72t does not apply to 401Ks directly. Remember, in using qualified programs the real concern along with market results, is the future taxation of these plans. If you are depositing money while in a 28% tax bracket, but paying 35%, 40%, or even 50% tax upon withdrawal, you have created a losing strategy.

IF SOMETHING YOU THOUGHT TO BE TRUE <u>WASN'T</u> TRUE,

WHEN WOULD YOU WANT TO KNOW ABOUT IT?

TRANSFER 4:

<u>MORTGAGES</u>
OWNING YOUR OWN HOME:
THE MOST MISUNDERSTOOD
AMERICAN DREAM

One of the largest transfers one will ever encounter is the purchasing of a home. It is part of the traditional American dream. It can turn into a nightmare with sleepless nights and difficult decisions. Obtaining the maximum amount of house with the minimum price is the obvious goal. Also, a must when considering a home purchase, are things such as neighbors, the neighborhood, schools, property taxes, city services, maintenance, and upkeep. When you finally find this castle, there is excitement in the air and a commitment to purchase. My friend, you are now entering into an unchartered universe, the twilight zone of the banking industry called the mortgage.

HELLO, I'M NEW ON THIS PLANET

All you know about the mortgage process is that you have worked your behind off, saved money for a down payment, and found a house you would like to buy. The next step, assuming you don't have your mattress stuffed with cash, is to try to get approved for a loan to purchase it. So you arrange to meet with your banker. Your first impression of the people in the mortgage department, is that on the outside they look just like you and me. They look friendly and seem polite. But underneath that normal exterior they serve only one master, the bank.

Their first apprisal of you is to decide whether to satisfy their needs of consumption. They want to see income statements, tax returns, lines of credit, and your credit scores. It's sort of funny that when you deposited $5,000 into one of their savings accounts they didn't ask you for any of this information. But let's face it, they just want to make sure you are not a credit risk. That's why, in the bank's eyes, every applicant is presumed to be a derelict and a liar. You must prove, beyond doubt, that you qualify financially so that you can afford any monetary abuse that they may throw at you. At the end of the first meeting, you sign an agreement allowing them to do this.

DIRT

Now as much as they <u>want</u> to give you a loan, by the time you walk to your car, they have started the process of making sure this won't be easy. The hunt is on for problems in your past. New or old, big or small they are fixed on the idea of finding any, and I mean <u>any</u>, financial problems you have had.

My personal experience is fairly common. I had purchased a home, sold it, and purchased another one. I lived in the new house about two years and decided to refinance it to lower the interest rate. All of these transactions were with the same bank and the same banker, all taking place in a seven year period. It was of no importance to them that I held several lines of credit with them with no debt balances and that my business account deposits with them were greater than the amount I wanted to refinance. At my expense, they wanted my credit scores and an appraisal of my home's value. The funny thing was, they had done this five months earlier for the other lines of credit I established with them. What a con game!

I'LL TAKE THE ONE ON THE BOTTOM

Your credit scores will vary from company to company. Some banks and mortgage companies will get as many as six or seven credit scores on you. Now, do you think they will use your best score? Guess again. How about the second or third best credit rating? Try again. How about the lowest or second to lowest score they can find? Bingo! Although five of your credit scores were good, they found the one they were looking for. In the bank's eyes you are now "one of those kind" of people.

NOT SO PERFECT

You get the phone call about your questionable credit scores but are told not to worry. They are going to work this out for you so you can have this dream house. You are told any additional costs will be handled at the closing. They are now in control.

Now, have you ever heard of a credit rating company making a mistake? Perhaps the rating companies information was incorrect and they record a low score, but the bank is going to use that one anyway. Chances of trying to correct any scores from a credit company in time for your closing are remote, it takes a long time.

WHAT FLAVOR WOULD YOU LIKE?

I am now entering into an area where you will really have to think from a different perspective. Home ownership and mortgages are confusing and emotional. As we discussed before, emotions are sometimes based on opinions not fact. I want to explore this confusion with you.

There is an array of different types of mortgages that you can select from. Banks and mortgage companies are becoming more creative in the packaging of these products. Why? They too see the ever-changing demographics of the country. They understand that buying a home is based on the affordability of the monthly payment, not necessarily the cost of the house. I can see how lending institutions would be considering extending the life of mortgages to 40 or 50 years. Why? More expensive homes, less future buyers of expensive homes, and retirees downsizing from larger homes. Banks and mortgage companies will want to create more buyers for these large homes while trying to maintain high values on these properties. The government also would like to see these larger homes maintain their values because this is a taxable commodity in the future. Property values continue to increase creating higher property taxes whether your house is paid off or not. The possible solutions for lending institutions would be to extend the payoff time of mortgages. Their thinking could be, "Hey, as long as we're collecting interest, why not?" The dilemma here is that no matter what type of mortgage you decide on, you will experience major wealth transfers. The solution to reducing these transfers is understanding the opportunities that lie inside the mortgage itself.

Types of mortgages vary. There are 15-year and 30-year mortgages, bi-weekly mortgages, interest-only mortgages, adjustable rate mortgages, and balloon mortgages that will assist you in paying off your house. There is also the old standby of simply paying cash for your home. No matter what you decide to do, transfers will occur. If you get a mortgage, you are paying interest to the lender (a transfer of your money), and if you pay cash not only do you lose the money that you paid for the house, but also the ability to earn more money from that money (lost opportunity cost).

Which of these two situations will cause the least amount of transfers for you? Many financial experts, along with your parents and grandparents, will conclude that paying your house off as fast as you can or paying cash for it, will result in the greatest rewards.

IF SOMETHING YOU THOUGHT TO BE TRUE, WASN'T TRUE. . .

Two lessons we talked about earlier come into play. Lost opportunity cost and liquidity, use, and control of your money will help you find the right solutions. By paying cash for your house, you must be of the belief that this is a great investment and you are certain of the rewards. After all, it's not everyday that you will plop down that kind of money on one investment. Experts will try to convince you that this is a wise decision. Let's take a look.

WATCH THE MONEY GROW? PAYING CASH

Lets assume you decided to pay cash for your home. You paid $150,000.00 cash for a house in an area where housing values grew. You bought the home six years ago and the current value of the home is now $200,000.00. You would look at that gain and conclude that your investment in your home netted $50,000.00. Simply put, that's over a 30% increase in the value of the home. So you go about telling all your friends how wise that decision was.

If you take the gain of $50,000.00 spread over six years, the real rate of return on that investment is 4.91%. The problem is during those six years, other payments were made to help increase the value of your property. New carpeting, painting, drapes, perhaps a new roof, furnace or air conditioner, possibly new windows and doors were improvements you made to increase the value of your home. Do not forget that you also pay property taxes that steadily increased with the value of your home.

Let's say that while you lived there you paid $2,000.00 a year in property taxes and paid $12,000.00 for improvements and maintenance. Over a six year period, that would be another $24,000.00 paid. The rate of return on your home, compounded annually, is now 2.35%. How does that compare to other investments available to you? In a down market, 2.35% sounds okay, but in a good market, that return sounds puny. Remember how everyone was impressed with your $50,000.00 gain?

NO MORE PAYMENTS???

I have to explain the financial implications when someone pays cash for their home. In exploring this idea, I need you to really think deeper financially than you ever had to before. The lessons of lost opportunity costs, liquidity, use, and control and the Rule of 72 must be applied to your thinking.

Most people think they will save interest by selecting a shorter loan period. With that in mind then paying cash for your home would save the most interest that would have normally been given to the bank. The problem is, by paying cash you no longer have that money to invest, so you are losing earnings that you could have made from that money. Also, if cash is paid for the house, you forfeit the tax benefits on the interest deduction. By using the tax deduction, you can recapture dollars, which you couldn't do had you paid cash. You must understand that it costs you the same amount of money to live in your house whether you have a mortgage or you paid cash. Let's take a look.

If you have a mortgage of $150,000.00 at 7% for 30 years, the monthly payment would be $997.95. If the monthly payment of $997.95 was invested for 30 years at 7% would equal $1,217,475.00. If, rather than paying $150,000.00 cash for the house, you invested it instead at 7% for 30 years, it would grow to $1,217,475.00. Presto, it's the same number!

Both of these scenarios are examples of transfers, whether you paid cash for your home or are making payments through a mortgage it is costing you money. The difference is that in the case of the 30 year mortgage at 7%, the mortgage would yield about $60,000.00 in tax savings in that 30 year period for someone in a 30% tax bracket. That is called recapturing some of your transfers.

15 vs. 30

The two most common types of mortgages sold today are the 15-year and 30-year mortgages. Once again, misinformation clouds the choice between these two types of mortgages. In the 15-year mortgages, people assume the shorter the loan period, the less they will have to pay. Secondly, they believe they will save interest payments. With this line of thinking, you must conclude that, once again, the best alternative would be paying cash for the house. Let's get out the microscope and take a look at these two mortgages.

Person A chose a 30-year mortgage for $150,000.00 with a 6.5% loan rate. She knows that under those terms her monthly payment will be $948.10. Person B obtained a 15-year mortgage for $150,000.00 with a 6.5% loan rate. He knows that his monthly payment for that loan will be $1,306.66.

Person A believes that her monthly payment at $948.10 is a good deal because it is $358.56 per month cheaper than the $1,306.66 payment for the 15-year mortgage. She is going to invest the savings of $358.56 per month into an account that averages a 6.5% return for 30 years. This grows to a tidy sum of $396,630.

Person B, who wasn't born yesterday, plans to save $1306.66 a month for 15 years after he makes the last payment on his 15-year mortgage. He too predicts a 6.5%

average return for those 15 years, and his investment would grow to an impressive $396,630.00. NOTE: It's the same amount as Person A's account. I have to ask you: Which person would you rather be?

In making the above comparison, I assumed a 6.5% mortgage loan rate and a 6.5% rate of return on their monthly payments. What would happen if both Persons A and B thought they could get an 8% average rate of return over that period of time on their investments? Person A's $358.56 per month for 30 years at 8% would grow to $534,382.00. Person B's $1,306.66 per month for 15 years would total $452,155 at an 8% earning rate. That's a difference of $82,227.00 in the favor of Person A. The compounding of interest works in Person A's account, causing the money to grow to a larger sum. Remember, Person B's banker told him he would save money with a 15-year mortgage.

Hold on there, Kemosabe. You're thinking, "If I took a 15 year mortgage, my interest rate might be lower than that 6.5% 30-year note." You're right. Let's say the interest rate was 6.0% on that 15-year mortgage. Then both Person A and Person B invested the difference at 8% return just as we described above. You're probably thinking, "Ah hah! Got you!" Try again. Person A's savings still ends up $35,697.00 greater than Person B's account. Don't forget, Person A also received 15 more years of tax deductions that created an even greater savings.

JIMMY CARTER

To continue our comparison of Persons A and B, we need to step into the WAYBAK time machine. Destination: the 1970's. It was a time of high inflation, hostages in Iran, and funny clothes. Mortgage rates were extremely high. It was not uncommon to see mortgage rates of 10%, 15%, 18%. To proceed with our comparison, we must agree that since interests rates have been much higher in the past than they are today, that it is possible for mortgage rates to go higher, and of course, possibly, lower. O.k., back to the WAYBAK machine. Destination: the present. Phew! What a trip!! I want to thank Mr. Carter for the lesson we learned.

Knowing that interest rates could go up or down, let's take a look at Persons A and B's 30- and 15-year mortgage. First of all, NOW READ THIS SLOWLY, there are more tax deductions in the first 15 years of a 30-year mortgage, than there are in the entire 15-year mortgage. Second, in Person A's 30-year mortgage, she knows for certain that her interest will remain the same for 30 years. Meanwhile, Person B's just made his last mortgage payment in the 15th year and is jubilant! My question is, now that he has paid off his mortgage, if he wanted to borrow money from his paid-off home, what are the interest rates? If he had a 15-year mortgage at 6.5%, and the interest rates are now 10%, you would have to say he was in a hurry to pay off his house at a lower rate so he could use his money at a higher rate. You see, Person A knows what her rate will be in that 16th year of a 30-year mortgage and because you put that $358.56 a month away, she now has accumulated $124,075.00 in savings by the

16th year. She has enough money to pay off her house at that time, IF SHE WANTS TO. If economic conditions are favorable to do that, she can. If the stock market is yielding higher rates of return, she may elect to continue to pay on her mortgage and let her savings grow. Now, in the 16th year, Person B is just starting his savings program. Which of these two people would you rather be now?

Most people would want to be Person A. Person A has more control and more options and opportunities in the future. She also has retained some liquidity, use and control of her money. This allows Person A to be more flexible in ever changing markets. Person A has also been able to maximize the tax deductions in the 30 year mortgage. Remember, taxes are the largest transfer of your wealth that you will see over your financial life. Recapturing your money in the form of tax deductions is important.

From the bank's standpoint, they would love to see everyone choose a 15-year mortgage. They will also encourage bi-weekly payments and any additional mortgage payments you can make. Why? These payments create the velocity of money for the bank. That means, the more money and the faster the money comes in, the more they can lend it out, to generate more profits. They disguise these payments as "interest saving techniques." **THINK ABOUT IT** . . .A bank, whose sole purpose is to collect interest, telling you how NOT to pay interest? It doesn't make sense.

CHANGING LANDSCAPE

Banks continue to tweak ideas about mortgages. It is their most lucrative product. The idea of interest-only mortgages is fairly new. In these mortgages you pay only the interest, no principal. They require you to put money into an account that the bank controls. An example would be, for every $100,000 you want to borrow you would put $12,500.00 into a 7% account controlled by the bank for 30 years. So, if you had an $200,000 home to finance, you would put $25,000 into their account. That money, the $25,000.00 at 7% would grow to meet a balloon payment due in the 30th year. Usually, the interest payments on this type of mortgage are higher than traditional mortgages.

Some mortgage companies tout a loan product that is totally flexible. You name the interest rate, and you name your monthly payment. They will tell you how many years it will take for you to pay it off. Hire a lawyer to read this contract. Of all these types of mortgages one thing stands out: The lending institutions are there to charge interest and make as much money as they can.

INSURING THE BANK

Most banks and mortgage companies require down payments. If you don't have a down payment they will charge you points. This extra money, above and beyond your mortgage payment, ensures them that in the event of foreclosure, their losses are covered. The standard down payment on a house is 20%. Again, the bank feels comfortable, because should you not make payments and they must foreclose on your home, that 20% covers their losses. I consider that a 20% up-front failure fee. Don't take it personally, they require this from almost everyone.

BLACK HOLE IN SPACE

Where does this down payment money go? If you were to put $30,000 down for your new home, what is your rate of return on the money? THINK HARD. ZERO! It will be zero percent forever. Next question: Can you borrow this $30,000.00 from the bank as part of your loan? NO! Why not? It's not part of the mortgage. Now, the banks will argue that it lowered your monthly payments. That may be true on the surface, but let's take a look at what the bank got out of this deal. They now have the use of your $30,000 for the next 30 years. At a 7.2% rate of return, that $30,000 would grow to $240,000 in 30 years for the bank. Just from the down payment they have earned more from you than what you paid for your house. Is your down payment deductible on your taxes? NO. Someone please remind me why I would want to do this. Remember, the bank is telling you the more you put down on the mortgage, the more you will save. Part of the solution to this problem is to demand that all of your down payment money be accessible to you through an equity line of credit.

I'VE HIT THE JACKPOT!

Meanwhile, back at the ranch . . . you just went through the meeting for the "closing" of your new home. You have signed 27 different documents, none of them which you understood. What the heck . . . if you can't trust the bank, who can you trust?

Now you're a homeowner. You think you're happy. The people at the bank gave you that congratulatory pen and calendar. They have truly put themselves in control of your future. They are happy. The people who sold the house to you are also happy. They even share their story of success with you. They bought that house new 33 years ago paying $39,000.00 for it. They remember how low the property taxes were back then, but even though they increased through the years, they still only averaged $1,000.00 a year in taxes. They remember the additions and improvements they made over the years totaling about $20,000.00. They feel it was their greatest investment. After all, they think they made $111,000.00 on the property.

THE MATH	
Sale Price	$150,000.
Original Purchase Price	($39,000.)
Gain on Sale	$111,000.
Years you owned the home	33

If you have a gain of $111,000.00 over 33 years, the annual compound rate of return is 4.17%. But what really happened was this:

THE MATH INCLUDING TAXES AND IMPROVEMENTS	
Sale Price	$150,000.
Original Purchase Price	($39,000.)
Taxes and Improvements (33 years)	($53,000.)
Gain on Sale	$58,000.
Years you owned the home	33

If you have a gain of $58,000.00 over 33 years, the annual compound interest return is 1.49%.

Now these people also had that house totally paid off for a few years. Had they been able to invest this $150,000 they had in the house, at a 7% earning rate they would have made $10,500 a year without touching the principal. That again is called a lost opportunity cost. The last three years they lived there they would have almost another $31,500.00 in lost opportunities. Plus, in losing the interest deductions, as little as they were, they became even more perfect taxpayers, which created more tax transfers of their wealth.

You congratulate them on their success, wish them well, and now you're asking yourself: Will you have the same success they did? After all, they were happy that they made such a huge profit on the sale of their house.

HOME EQUITY

If you have accumulated equity in your home, let me ask you one question: What's the rate of return on the equity built up in your house? I mean, if you built up $70,000 of equity in your home, the bank must be sending you a hefty dividend check, right? WRONG! The equity inside your house is growing at <u>zero</u> percent. The argument here is, "Well my house increased in value therefore, my equity went up." Well, whether you have $70,000.00 or $1.00 of equity, the value of your property would still have gone up. If property values went down, would you rather lose $1.00 or $70,000.00 of equity? Although we have been taught that our home is a safe place to park our money, we really have to take a look at this situation.

WHO IS IN CONTROL?

It is important for you to understand how to get liquidity, use and control of the equity in your home. This is not money that you would invest, gamble, or spend foolishly. But, it can open up a great number of opportunities for you in the future.

BE THE BANK

If you do have equity in your house, it is important that you establish an equity line of credit. Be advised, this is NOT used for investing. This credit line should be used to establish your own personal "bank." Current tax laws may allow you to deduct the interest paid on your equity line of credit. Consult with your accountant to make sure you qualify for these interest deductions. Under most mortgage situations you will. The government really doesn't care what you purchase with your equity line of credit. You will receive an interest paid statements from the bank at the end of the year. It is similar to your mortgage interest statement. The rate of interest on equity line of credit may even be lower than your mortgage interest rate.

As previously stated, an equity line of credit should not be used to make investments, but can be used to eliminate interest payments that are not deductible. If you could take $5,000.00 of credit card debt at 18% with a $300.00 monthly payment and reduce it to a 6% interest rate with a $100.00 monthly payment and be able to deduct the interest off your taxes, would you be interested? That's what an equity line of credit can do for you. If you have $12,000.00 balance on your car loan and you are paying $350.00 a month for it, how would you like to pay $250.00 a month and deduct the interest from that loan off your taxes? As you can see, there are many ways this could be favorable to you.

TAX FREE MONEY

The equity inside our homes, under current tax law, is tax-free money. Now, I don't know what they were smoking when they passed that law, but whatever it was, I'd like to send them some more. But, there are also things that could negatively impact the tax-free equity in your home.

HELLO BUBBA!

You're sitting in your home, looking out the window at the new landscaping project you just completed. There's a knock at your front door. There, standing on your porch, is a guy you have never seen before. You crack the door open and he says:

"Howdy! My name is Bubba. I'm your new neighbor. I've got six dogs, their all pretty friendly except for that one with no hair. . . if I were you I wouldn't try to pet him. I've got four kids. Aren't kids a hoot? I'll tell you, between parole officers and social workers, kids sure keep you busy. My wife, now there's a fine woman. You might see her from time to time. She's gonna re-upholster furniture right out there on the front porch, to make extra money. Me, why I'm a work at home kinda guy. I'll be rebuilding truck engines right here in the driveway. If you ever need my help, just let me know. See you, buddy!"

This is more like, see you property values. Now, that example may seem a little extreme, but such a neighbor would dramatically affect the value of your house, and the tax-free equity in your home. Even just some neighbor who didn't maintain their property very well could effect your values.

Once, while my wife and I were searching for a home, we found a property that we really liked. I happened to walk out into the back yard and a little dog next door started barking. Barking and barking, followed by more and more barking. I looked at the real estate person and said they would have to lower the price of the house quite a bit if I was going to spend the rest of my life trying to convince that dog to be quiet. What is the price of peace and quiet in your own backyard?

FEDERAL RESERVE

Another situation that effects your tax free equity in your home is the Federal Reserve. The Fed set the interest rates that affect the bank loan rates. Your ability to afford a house is based on your ability to make that monthly payment. If interest rates were low, housing values are high.   Because less of the monthly payment goes to interest. If interest rates rise, home values fall. More money, on a monthly basis, would have to go to interest. The seller might have to lower the price of the house so that it is affordable, on a monthly basis, to attract buyers. Remember Jimmy Carter, interest rates skyrocketed, housing values plummeted. There goes the house values and the tax free equity again.

YOU'RE DEAD

We're just pretending here, but if you and your spouse die in a common accident, what becomes of the tax free equity in your home? It can magically become taxable again, this time at a higher rate, in your estate. Let's review quickly: You're breathing, it's tax free; You're not breathing, it may be taxable! Enough said.

NOT DEAD, JUST DISABLED

We just discussed situations that could affect your home's value, and affect that tax-free equity that's earning a whopping zero percent. Without liquidity, use and control of this equity you may also be facing another danger. Let's say one of the bread winners in a household is involved in an accident or has a mild heart attack and survives. Now medical insurance covered most things, but the on-going therapy isn't covered. The spouse, needing financial help, goes down to see the friendly banker for help. "I need some of the $70,000.00 equity I have in my home for medical reasons." The banker musters up enough dignity and tells the spouse this: "Unfortunately, your mortgage payments were based on two income earners, not one. We feel you don't have the ability to pay back (YOUR) tax-free equity to us with interest. Thank you, good luck."

48 percent of all foreclosures in the United States are caused by a disability. Having proper liquidity, use and control of your money would prevent some financial calamities.

3000 DAYS

When it comes to your home, the country's demographics could play an important role. At a time when builders are building mega-homes for $300,000.00 to $500,000.00, we have to take a look at our aging population. With two-thirds of the now-working population 60 years old or older in 3000 days, consider this: A large portion of the population will be downsizing their homes. As people get older, they don't need these 6000 square foot homes. Keeping up the payments and maintenance of these mega-homes will be a drain on retirement incomes. There may be a time when there is an over-abundance of these homes on the market. Prices lowered to attract more buyers, means loss of home values and lower equity values in the house. Once again, it's not a good place for your money to be when experiencing a down housing market.

SOLUTIONS

We have discussed the many aspects of home ownership and mortgages. It is important to establish as much liquidity, use and control of your money as possible. As previously discussed, a 30-year mortgage is more favorable than most other options. Further, you should limit the amount of down payment paid at purchase as much as possible. Establishing an equity line of credit on your home can give you liquidity, use and control of your equity. Refrain from paying cash for your home, as neighbors, interest rates, property taxes, and death taxes affect the value of your home. You create unintended consequences when you live in a home that is paid-off, without understanding your options. Failing to understand your options leads to lost opportunity costs, which in turn will create major transfers of your wealth.

PAYING YOURSELF BACK -
THE VELOCITY OF MONEY

If you are the owner of your "bank," your equity line of credit, you have created liquidity, use and control of your money. If you purchased a car for $25,000.00 at 5% interest for 48 months, the payments would be $575.13 a month. You borrow the money from your "bank" to buy the car, and pay yourself back the $575.13 a month for 48 months. What happened here? You charged yourself the loan company interest rate, replaced the money into your "bank" in 4 years, and took tax deductions on the interest. After 4 years, the money has been replaced and it's time to buy another car with the same money. There is still some value in the old car to assist you on your next purchase, possibly $6,000.00 or $7,000.00. Does it feel a little better being the owner of the "bank?"   Remember, a car is a depreciating asset. Paying cash up front on something that will lose money is a losing strategy.

OUR GOAL

The objective of these exercises is to show you how to take back the liquidity, use, and control of your money.

Unintended Consequences:
The Transfers

We also want to reduce or eliminate transfers of your money that are unnecessary. Recognizing these transfers and dealing with them can save you thousands of dollars. We want to create other "banks" of money for you that are tax efficient and help you retain monetary control. We will create these other "banks" by using the money you saved when you have eliminated and reduced unnecessary transfers of your wealth. Thus, you will not spend one more dime than you are already spending. By doing this, you will have more knowledge and money to make better financial decisions that profit you, not others. This will be an exciting change in the way you think about money!

IT IS DIFFICULT TO GET THE RIGHT SOLUTIONS WHEN YOU START WITH THE WRONG PREMISE

TRANSFER 5:

<u>FINANCIAL PLANNING</u>

As we established early on, the American public is bombarded by the media, bullied by sales people and bewildered by the things it feels it needs to know. When it comes to finances, this is the confusion most people face. A lot of the conflict is created by several industries trying to profit under the guise of trying to help people financially. They provide product and or services, both of which are for sale. Banks, investment firms, insurance companies, money managers, brokers, financial planners, lawyers and accountants, all want your financial attention. All profess to have all the solutions to all your financial concerns. Who's right and who's wrong?

Most of these industries will try to convince you that the competition is inept, incompetent and incomplete. The best defense is a good offense and these industries are very busy trying to dismember their competition in front of potential clients. You can cut their arrogance with a knife. Don't get me wrong, there are a lot of highly skilled professional people out there, but they find it impossible to think beyond their own industry. A lot of their training and background will narrowly point their clients in one direction. If anyone suggests anything other than that one direction, they will be labeled as crazy. Thus, the confusion!

All of these industries are motivated by one thing. Money, more specifically, YOUR MONEY! These industries make money via fees, commissions, management and expense charges. They will always profess that "the other guy is ripping you off." It is disappointing and unprofessional that the people in this industry are willing to put the client (you) in the middle of these arguments.

You must find someone who knows and understands transfers of your wealth. If you don't, these groups will be simply asking you to give up some of your standard of living to fund their projects and programs. Without knowledge, you will remain bewildered.

Remember, these industries and salespeople believe that there is only one way to make your money grow: Through higher rates of return. Again, when chasing higher rates of return, who is the one at risk, you or the one making the recommendation? In a down market, who wins, you or them? If you discover transfers of your wealth and reduce them, your wealth would grow regardless of market performance. I call that growth *internal savings.* Let's take a look at some different types of planning and savings concepts available to the public, compared to internal savings.

INVESTMENT FUND [IF]

$80,000	Deposits
$6,000	Earnings
$4,800	Earnings After Taxes
Yes	Fees

BANK SAVINGS [BS]

$150,000	Deposits
$6,000	Earnings
$4,800	Earnings After Taxes
Yes	Fees

INTERNAL SAVINGS [IS]

$0	Deposits
$6,000	Earnings
$6,000	Earnings After Taxes
No	Fees

IF

In interviewing financial professionals, you are looking for someone who could best fulfill your financial needs. First, the investment fund (IF) salespeople say you could earn $6,000.00 in one of their accounts. You would have had to deposit $80,000.00 in the account. Unfortunately, you would have to pay capital gains tax on the growth and you would end up with net earnings of $4,800. There may also be advisory fees and account fees, based on your account balances and the type of account it is.

BS

Banks also want your business, so they introduce you to their bank savings (BS) programs. The bank says it too could get you a $6,000.00 return. All you would have to do is to put $150,000.00 into their handy dandy CD account. Of course, you would have to pay capital gains tax on your earnings, leaving you with $4,800.00. There may also be some fees charged annually to maintain this account, in addition to penalties if you want or need to withdraw some of that money before its maturity date.

IS

Now I come along and tell you about internal savings (IS) and teach you about transfers that you unknowingly and unnecessarily make every day. I say I can also get you a $6,000.00 return. The big difference is, you don't need to deposit any money in any account. Even more rewarding, there will be no tax on your gain and no fees or penalties involved. Finally, the coup de grace: This is the only program where the $6,000.00 is guaranteed.

Now ask yourself: Do you want your financial future based on IF, BS, or something you know IS going to happen? Internal savings, by reducing transfers, also teaches the lessons needed to end the confusion that all the financial industries create. Remember, someone earning $75,000.00 a year, saving $5,000.00 of that income, would have $70,000.00 in residual income to pay all their bills and taxes. If you could internally save 1% of that $70,000.00, you would create a 14% increase on your $5,000 savings, with no market risk, fees, penalties or spending one more dime out of your pocket. Does this sound like the type of financial advice and planning you would like to pursue?

In the comparison, you will notice that by utilizing internal savings and reducing transfers, you can increase your lifestyle and standard of living money. You may also be able to enhance your own "banks" and create more liquidity, use and control of your money, in addition to benefitting from significant tax savings. Converting transfers to internal savings will bring about that defining moment in the way you think about money.

As I stated previously, I don't believe the way in which financial planning is being sold to the American public. There <u>are</u> good people out there to help you, but finding them is the trick. Measure them on their experience and knowledge. Make sure they surround themselves with other professionals and specialists and preferably you were referred to them by someone you know and trust. Find someone who continues the process of teaching you financial techniques you need to know and can use.

INTERNAL SAVINGS: AN EXAMPLE

We have talked about transfers of your wealth and how they affect you. Let's take a look at how learning about dealing with transfers, and recapturing transferred dollars could change your life.

I met a 40 year old woman who was totally depressed about work, saving money, and spending money. But her main concern was she wanted to create the best possible learning atmosphere for her daughter by sending her to a private school. The problem was that in her current lifestyle, she felt there was no way she could afford the $450.00 monthly tuition needed to enroll her daughter in private school. After all, like most households, there was no EXTRA MONEY left over at the end of the year to do anything. Look up "EXTRA MONEY" in Webster's dictionary. It doesn't exist.

Unintended Consequences:
The Transfers

I told her that I believed it was possible to send her daughter to that private school WITHOUT her spending one more dime than she was already spending. Her look of disbelief told me that she had gone through her share of other planners' quick fixes. I could sense her reluctance but assured her that she would experience a defining moment in the way she looked at her finances. I told her that after one meeting she would learn more about finances than she had her entire life, and with this knowledge she could enroll her daughter into the private school without spending any more money. She said prove it! So I set about doing just that.

HER STATS
- 40 years old, single mom, divorced
- One child, 11 year old daughter
- $45,000 gross income per year
- Homeowner   30 year mortgage at 7%
                         13 years left on mortgage
- 28% tax bracket

HER INITIAL GOAL

- Enroll her daughter in private school, now through high school (7 years)
- Get control of her finances
- Maintain current lifestyle
- There was no money after taxes to do this.

HER BASIC LIFESTYLE	
Home Value	$180,000.
Mortgage Balance	$60,000.
Home Equity Value	$120,000.
401(k) Balance	$50,000.
Mutual Funds	$20,000.
Bank Savings	$10,000.
Average Annual Tax Refund	$4,000.
Credit Card Debt	$3,000.
Car Debt	$11,000.

Upon seeing these figures, I knew she could improve her situation greatly. But, her concern was there was no money left at the end of each month. I told her we would take a look at her monthly outlay, and possibly, we could find some answers there.

HER BASIC LIFESTYLE		Monthly Payment
Home Value	$180,000.	
Mortgage Balance	$60,000.	$1,000.
Home Equity Value	$120,000.	
401(k) Balance	$50,000.	$400.
Mutual Funds	$20,000.	$100.
Bank Savings	$10,000.	$0.
Average Annual Tax Refund	$4,000.	$0.
Credit Card Debt	$3,000.	$150.
Car Debt	$11,000.	$350.
MONTHLY OUTLAY		**$2,000.**

While I could see the problem, she couldn't. First of all, she was convinced by her parents and the mortgage lender to reduce her debt on the house as fast as she could. You've already learned the folly of paying off one's house prematurely. Next, her accountant told her to put almost 10% of her salary into her 401(k), despite the fact that her employer matched only 5% of her salary. You've also learned that savings in these qualified plans is not real, but only apparent. Finally, the last financial planner she talked to convinced her that all her problems could be solved by investing $100.00 a month into a mutual fund. Overall, her debt seemed relatively average.

Unintended Consequences:
The Transfers

START THINKING

What I really needed for her to do was to start thinking. She said, "See, I'm laying out $2,000.00 a month, and that doesn't cover food, clothes and what little luxuries we have." She was afraid if anything happened to her, she could lose everything. She was right. I saw that her fears had crippled her from making necessary financial decisions.

She needed to look at things from a different perspective. The next few minutes would be critical. I said, "Ok, we know what your monthly payments are, but what is the rate of return on the equity in your home?" She looked at me sort of puzzled and said, "Well the value of my house has gone up, but I don't know the percentage." I told her she was correct, the value of her property did go up. I asked her whether her property value would have gone up whether she had $1.00 or $120,000.00 of equity in the house. YES, it would have gone up. The question again was regarding the rate of return on her home equity of $120,000.00? The answer is ZERO!!!

LIFESTYLE			
		Monthly Payment	**Rate of Return**
Home Value	$180,000.		
Mortgage Balance	$60,000.	$1,000.	
Home Equity Value	$120,000.		0%
Home Down Payment	$30,000.		

I asked her, "Remember putting that $30,000.00 down on your home at purchase? Well, what has been the rate of return on that $30,000.00?" She looked at me quizzically asked, "Zero?" I said, "My, you're getting smart. You're right, there is no rate of return on that money." At this point, I had to ask her one more question. "If you needed that $30,000.00 for an emergency, could you borrow it from the bank?" She just stared at me. I said, "No, because it's not part of the mortgage."

LIFESTYLE			
		Monthly Payment	**Rate of Return**
Home Value	$180,000.		
Mortgage Balance	$60,000.	$1,000.	
Home Equity Value	$120,000.		0%
Home Down Payment	$30,000.		0%

LIFESTYLE SAVINGS

I continued by asking her about her savings, and I congratulated her on her attempt to save money. She had money accumulated in the bank, in a 401(k), and in mutual funds. When I asked her how she felt about her savings, she said she felt confused and troubled. She said she was losing money faster than she could invest it. I told her that she was not alone and this market confounded even the so-called experts. Over the last three years, she had received the standard professional advice, "Keep doing what you were doing, it will get better." I asked, "I know your putting in $400.00 a month into your 401(k), but what has been the rate of return on it the last couple of years?" She sighed and said, "I've lost about 15% a year." She also stated right away that her mutual fund return was better than that. She had only lost 10% the year before (2000 to 2002 time frame). I congratulated her, and she laughed and said, "But I'm getting 2% return from the bank CD." It was time to celebrate.

HOPE FOR RECOVERY?

I told her, as funny as it might sound, she was in a good position, she just didn't know it. Let's take a look at her money and see.

LIFESTYLE			
		Monthly Payment	**Rate of Return**
Home Value	$180,000.		
Mortgage Balance	$60,000.	$1,000.	
Home Equity Value	$120,000.		0%
Home Down Payment	$30,000.		0%
401(k)	$50,000.	$400.	-15%
Mutual Funds	$20,000.	$100.	-10%
Bank Savings	$10,000.	$0.	2%
Annual Tax Refund	$4,000.	$0.	0%

She said, "I don't see anything good here." I told her between her home and savings she had invested a total of $230,000.00. If you look at her rates of return, anybody would be depressed. I asked her, "Did the people handling your accounts at the bank or investment company ever call you to try to help you?" "NO," she said firmly. "Did you call them?" "NO," she said.

"One more thing," I added, "What was the rate of return that the government gave you for that over payment of taxes you sent them?" She said, "Let me guess, ZERO?" Yup! I looked at her and said that her debt was in line with her income. I asked her, "Are you ready to save some money so you can put your daughter in that private school? Let's get to work."

HOME SWEET HOME

First, I reviewed how she was dealing with her home. She had a $60,000.00 mortgage balance with 13 years of payments left. Her $997.95 monthly payment carries a 7% interest rate. This means she had $156,000.00 ($1,000 x 12 months x 13 years) in payments left. If she would consider refinancing the balance on the home it would make a big difference. Her $60,000.00 balance refinanced at 6.5% for 30 years would create a monthly payment of $380.00. That's a $620.00 per month difference in what she was currently paying. She looked at me and asked, "Won't I be paying more over the 30 years in payments?" I said, "Let's find out. If you paid $380.00 a month for 30 years you have $136,800.00 in payments compared to the $156,000.00 payments due in your current situation." I then asked her if she could use an extra $620.00 a month. She didn't have to think about that one.

FUTURE CONCERNS

I told her that she might feel content just refinancing her house. The $620.00 per month was more than enough savings to put her daughter into her school of choice. But, she wanted to continue to see what else could be done. So we looked at her attempts at saving for her future. She had a 401(k) into which she was depositing $400.00 per month and her employer was matching these savings up to $200.00 per month. She had experienced negative returns on this account for the past three years. If she were only to deposit up to what the employer was matching in the 401(k). I told her, as I mentioned in earlier chapters, that I had reservations whether a 401(k) would create real tax savings in the future for her. By reducing her 401(k) contribution to the matching amount, she would save an additional $200.00 per month. As for the mutual funds, I advised her to stop investing $100.00 per month in a losing market. This money could also help fund her daughters education for that seven year period.

She said, "That sounds good, but what will happen to my retirement savings?" I told her that if she added no more money to her 401(k) and received an average of a 7% rate of return, it would grow to $286,270.00 in 25 years. Also, should she continue to deposit $200.00 per month in addition to her employer's match, at 7% that monthly amount will grow to another $325,918.00 by the time she reached age 65. Those two amounts add up to $612,188.00 in her 401(k). In addition, without depositing any further funds, the mutual funds at an average rate of return of 7%, would grow to $114,508.00 by age 65. Total all that up and it comes to $726,696.00 at age 65. I admonished that these are not guaranteed returns and the amounts used in my example could vary dramatically. However, with $726,696.00, she could live on $60,000.00 at 7% for 24 years and that's not including social security, if it's still around.

SPENDING DOWN AN ASSET

She seemed less depressed as we talked. I asked "Have you ever spent down an asset?" She didn't know what I meant so I explained, "If you took the $10,000.00 you have in the bank and withdrew $150.00 a month until it was gone, that would be spending down an asset. How long would it take for that money to be done?" She shrugged her shoulders. I told her that at 7% it would last 7 years. "Isn't that the number of years you need to fund your daughter's education?" She shook her head, YES!

TAX EXUBERANCE

Now, of all the things that are misunderstood, receiving a large tax refund every year, takes the top prize. Remember, the government isn't paying you any interest on this money. That $4,000 refund represents $333.00 per month out of her pocket. When I told her that it was almost enough to make her car payment, she said she never thought of it that way. I looked at her and said, "Remember thinking is mandatory."

WELL LOOKY HERE

Now we took a look at her financial picture if she did the things we discussed:

LIFESTYLE				
	Value	Monthly Payment	Rate of Return	New Monthly Payment
Home Value	$180,000.			
Mortgage Balance	$60,000.	$1,000.		$380.
Home Equity Value	$120,000.		0%	
Home Down Payment	$30,000.		0%	
401(k)	$50,000.	$400.	-15%	$200.
Mutual Funds	$20,000.	$100.	-10%	$0.
Bank Savings	$10,000.	$0.	2%	$0.
Annual Tax Refund	$4,000.	$0.	0%	$0.
Credit Card Debt	$3,000.	$150.		$150.
Car Debt	$11,000.	$350.		$350.
MONTHLY OUTLAY		**$2,000.**		**$1,080.**

Her original monthly expenditures were $2,000.00, but after a little thinking, it has been reduced to $1,080.00 per month. A $920.00 per month savings!

BUT LOOK AGAIN

If she were to spend down the $10,000.00 in bank savings over seven years, she would offset that $1,080.00 per month even more. To further reduce that monthly outlay, I told her to call the Human Resources department of her employer, and have them adjust her exemptions so she wouldn't continue to overpay her taxes. If done properly, she could pick up another $300.00 per month, and eliminate that large refund.

By spending down the $10,000.00 and changing her withholding, she saved a total of $450.00 per month. Subtracting that from her new monthly outlay of $1,080.00, and her new adjusted monthly outlay is $630.00. That's a $1,370.00 per month difference. I asked her, "Do you feel you can afford that private school now?"

ARE WE THERE YET?

I told her, "I know this has been a long journey. We are almost there. But, I want you to look one more time. This time, I want to look at your debt." She said, "Ok."

Between the credit card debt and the car loan, she was paying about $500.00 per month in payments. I asked,

Unintended Consequences:
The Transfers

"Would you be interested in reducing that monthly payment by over 30%? Would you also like to deduct the interest you are paying for this debt from your taxes?" I reminded here that when we first started talking about refinancing her home, I had mentioned an equity line of credit. If she were to establish an equity line of credit, she could use it to pay off her car note and credit card balances. She was paying 18% interest on her credit card and 7% on the car loan. By using an equity line of credit, she could lower the interest rate to approximately 5%. This interest rate would be flexible, and her new monthly payment on the credit card would go from $150.00 to $75.00 per month. Her car payment would be reduced from $350.00 to $247.00 per month. The interest on these loans would then be tax deductible and she would save another $100.00 per year in tax savings. She said, "Great!"

I said to her, "I really believe you will start to enjoy your life more now that you have created some financial freedom for yourself. Gaining liquidity, use and control of your money creates that freedom. Obviously, I still have concerns that we must address when it comes to protecting your assets. In the event of something happening to you, I would want you to receive an income. As a single parent, this is very important."

LIFESTYLE					
	Value	Monthly Payment	Rate of Return	New Monthly Payment	Spend Down Asset
Home Value	$180,000.				
Mortgage Balance	$60,000.	$1,000.		$380.	
Home Equity Value	$120,000.		0%		
Home Down Payment	$30,000.		0%		
401(k)	$50,000.	$400.	-15%	$200.	
Mutual Funds	$20,000.	$100.	-10%	$0.	
Bank Savings	$10,000.	$0.	2%	$0.	$150.
Annual Tax Refund	$4,000.	$0.	0%	$0.	$300.
Credit Card Debt	$3,000.	$150.		$75.	
Car Debt	$11,000.	$350.		$247.	
MONTHLY OUTLAY		**$2,000.**		**$902.**	
SPEND DOWN ASSET				**($450.)**	
NEW MONTHLY OUTLAY				**$452.**	

Original Monthly Outlay:	$2,000.
New Monthly Outlay:	$ 452.
Internal Savings - Difference	$1,548.

"If you recall, we were originally be looking for $450.00 per month to send your daughter to private school, but we found an additional $1,098.00 of savings. Can you see the power of recapturing transfers that you're currently making? Did you feel that defining moment in the way you think about your money?" The client was ecstatic, and had indeed felt that defining moment.

If you have the knowledge to deal with the transfers of your wealth and learn to recapture money you are unknowingly and unnecessarily spending, it will truly change your life. **WITHOUT SPENDING ONE MORE DIME. PLEASE NOTE THAT NO PRODUCT PURCHASE WAS NECESSARY.**

We set a time to start working on her lifestyle. You couldn't believe how happy she was. She thanked me, thanked me and thanked me. For a moment I almost felt special. My reward was changing her ability to think, which changed her life, and changed her daughter's future.

In the foregoing example, there was a lot of work that had to be done. Aside from refinancing the home, there were additional things that had to be considered such as what to do with the extra money, and how to curtail her exposure in the event of disability. It would be devastating for her to lose her ability to earn an income. Everything she worked for would be gone if she was disabled for any length of time. In the event of her death, heaven forbid, work had to be done to provide direction for her wealth and her daughter's future.

ON TRIAL: FINANCIAL BELIEFS

What is on trial here is a belief system: The fast paced, get-rich-while-you-can mentality, where the solution is based upon products, not knowledge. There is nothing wrong with most investment products, but products are not the only answer to securing your financial future. We have become so mesmerized by rates of return, we fail to use common sense, which costs us a lot of money. Have we become so busy that we just look the other way when giving away our money? I believe we have been systematically trained to do just that. From our education system, to banks, brokers, investment companies, the government to tax preparers, we are told very little about how to manage our personal finances. But we are blindly guided down this narrow path and eventually left hanging out to dry, for one reason and one reason only: So that others can profit.

RELYING ON STUPIDITY

I can't blame these institutions and companies for wanting profits. If the public is willing to freely give away their money, then more power to them. No one is being forced to do anything. The concept of making money out of nothing is ingenious. Motivated by the emotions of fear and greed, love and hate, people will freely throw money away. If anyone dare throw common sense into this mix, they would probably be labeled as cold and calculating. As long as people are willing to give their money away, someone will take it. One thing I am positive of: this will never change. PT Barnum said it best, "There's a sucker born every minute." People have been duped so long, they are afraid of change in the fear of being duped again. The only thing that will stop this madness is knowledge. Until that happens, billions of dollars will be made from us, the public, by simply relying on our stupidity.

FINANCIAL PUPPETS

Because of this lack of knowledge, you will, willingly or unwillingly, stay financially tied to these institutions for the rest of your life. The money you will transfer away is enormous. Reducing these transfers will help create personal wealth for you. Achieving some financial freedom in your life should be a personal goal. If financial institutions had their way, you would remain captive to them forever. For that reason, they don't want to educate you too much. Rather, they want to create a dependency on them.

<u>POVERTY PLANNING:</u>
IT TAKES NO TIME
IT TAKES NO EFFORT
RESULTS*ARE GUARANTEED
*Results may vary depending on luck

All too often I see people doing the very basics, financially. Their heads buried in the sand, they take the ostrich approach to planning. The "wait-and-see" retirement strategy suits them well. Then, with this limited or non-existent knowledge, they attempt to survive in a world created for them by the government. They have been told that their pension and retirement saving will be enough to live on in their golden years. Let us not forget social security. But the ever-increasing cost of living, increased taxation and increased cost of insurance, drains the basics of their planning away. They all too often end up looking for part-time jobs after retirement. Pride, fear, and laziness fuel the ignorance of poverty planning. They received financial advice from their friends and neighbors, but remain skeptical of anyone with professional knowledge. They work and work and never get ahead. Unfortunately, these are the same financial lessons they pass on to their children.

I DON'T MIND DYING, I JUST DON'T WANT TO BE THERE WHEN IT HAPPENS.

TRANSFER 6:

<u>INSURANCE</u>

If something has no value don't insure it! The insurance industry is one of the few industries that has created more confusion than clarity.

LIFE & DEATH

What would you call someone, who lived a couple of houses down from you, that in the middle of the night, left his wife and three kids? He left them with no means of support and a lot of debt. What adjective would describe this person?

What would you call someone, who in the middle of the night, died, and left his family with no means of support and a lot debt. The adjectives would be a little different, but the results would be exactly the same.

Now, if we took the same scenario and said he died in the middle of the night, but left his family a large life insurance policy, what would you call him? A loving husband and father? That gift of love to his wife and kids expressed that his commitment to his family did not end with his last breath, but lived on into the future. He was there in sickness and in health, in life and in death.

I know this is a sensitive subject and it isn't fun to talk about, but it is an important subject and in many cases misunderstood. Once again, I'm going to ask you to think a layer deeper on this topic. What you hear about life insurance from others, may not necessarily be true. Advice you received about life insurance may be based more on opinion rather than fact. Insurance companies that produce these products will always profess to be the best. Have you ever seen an advertisement where a company stated that their product is mediocre? There are good products and bad products out there, so marketing that is based on price of the life insurance, is flawed. Cheaper is <u>not</u> better, in most cases. If you used that philosophy for everything you bought you would end up with a house full of junk. I have seen a lot of competition based on price, but very little on the provisions of the insurance contracts.

HODGEPODGE OF POLICIES

An insurance contract is a legal document, an agreement to pay benefits in the event of loss, in exchange for a premium. There are many different types of policies available to the public. There are universal life, variable life, whole life, survivor life, modified whole life, blended whole life, term life, decreasing term, increasing yearly term, etc. The creative list goes on and on. To add to the confusion, each company's policy provisions may be different for each of these types of policies. No wonder consumers cringe when they hear the words "life insurance."

CASH VALUE

I could spend several boring weeks explaining different types of life insurance. I don't want to do that, however I do want to address the concept of cash value life insurance compared to term insurance. Cash value insurance policies build up values inside the contract either through the payments of dividends, interest rates or investment returns. Over a period of time, these values could add up to a tidy sum. It is frowned upon to call this an investment vehicle, but you can't ignore the fact that policy values, if used properly, are a valuable financial asset.

Term insurance policies are bought for a specific term of time. The most common term lengths are ten, fifteen and twenty year policies. Term insurance builds up no cash value. Some companies profess to have some cash value term. In most cases though, there are no values in these policies. The insurance company needs not set aside any cash reserves for term, resulting in the policies being sold at a much cheaper premium than cash value policies.

INSURANCE TRANSFERS OF YOUR WEALTH

No matter how you think about it or what type of policy you buy, you will transfer dollars to pay premiums. The decision you make whether you buy cash value insurance or term insurance could be a costly one. If you could recapture the dollars you will pay in premiums on a policy, would you do it? In the end, life insurance can provide options and opportunities and can resolve a number of financial problems at one time. Life insurance creates protection, monetary value, and can have favorable income tax and estate tax results. Learning to use your policy is as important as buying it.

HOW MUCH IS ENOUGH?
"CLEAN UP IN AISLE FOUR!"

Determining the amount of insurance one should have is a major issue. You will get different answers from different professionals. It's amazing to me how one evaluates ones life value. Let's say you own life insurance with a death benefit of $100,000.00. You assumed, for reasons no one can explain, that it was a sufficient amount. While you are shopping at the grocery store, a condenser in the frozen food section explodes, leaving you and two hundred pounds of prime beef spread all over the place, i.e. you're dead. Your family hires an attorney to sue the store. The value of your prematurely-ended life, in the court case, is determined to be $10 million dollars. Now, that is a pretty wide spread between what you thought your life was worth compared to what the attorneys and judge thought. Your family is happier with their evaluation than yours.

SELF-INFLICTED TAX

I have seen it happen. People will go on the Internet and buy one million dollars worth of term insurance, not knowing they may have just created an estate tax problem for themselves. If the proper estate planning is not done, the death benefit of the policy could be included as part of your estate. Before you bought that policy, you may not have had to pay Estate taxes, but now with the value of the policy added in, you created a mess.

BUY TERM AND INVEST THE DIFFERENCE?

The most common marketing ploy for term insurance tells us to buy term insurance rather than cash value insurance and invest the difference. If that's such sound advice, why don't we apply the wisdom more often? For example: Buy folding chairs, not a couch, and invest the difference. Buy a push mower, not a power mower, and invest the difference. Buy a bicycle, not a car, invest the difference. Buy a shovel, not a snow blower, invest the difference. Buy a pet, don't have kids, invest the difference. Buy scissors, cut your own hair, invest the difference. Buy just aspirin, not your prescriptions, invest the difference. Stay at home, don't take the spouse out, invest the difference. Move back in with your parents, sell your house, invest the difference. Visit the mall, instead of taking a vacation, invest the difference. It seems this philosophy works with everything! Simply, extract value, and invest the difference.

The marketing of term insurance is an art form in itself. From the internet, banks, television deals and mass mailings, to auto insurers, mortgage companies and brokerage houses, it seems to be very popular. Why? Well, here are the term insurance facts. Less than one policy in ten survives the term for which it was written.[15] The average life span of a term policy before termination

---

[15]Penn State University, 1993 Study on the Fate of Term Insurance Policy.

or conversion is 2 years.[16] 45% of all term policies are terminated or converted in the first year.[17] 72% of all term policies are terminated or converted in the first three years.[18] Finally, and the most glaring statistic is that only 1% of all term policies result in a death claim.[19] Insurance companies love term policies, and clearly term policies are very profitable for them. So they market the heck out of these policies with little fear of having to pay out death benefits.

IF THERE IS MONEY TO BE MADE. . .

Investment people, accumulators, those who invest your money for you and charge a fee also want you to buy term insurance. It stands to reason they want you to spend less on everything so you can invest the difference with them, so they can make more money. Regardless of the statistics on term insurance, they will tell you it's the wise thing to do. Banks also push term insurance. Much like the accumulators, they don't want you to spend too much money on insurance because they are afraid they will lose money that would normally flow into savings and CD accounts.

---

[16]*Id.*

[17]*Id.*

[18]*Id.*

[19]*Id.*

You can see why there is such a ground swell of support for term insurance. It's called PROFITS! Their profits, not yours.

LET'S DO SOME MORE MATH!

It would be reasonable to say that renting an apartment would be cheaper than buying a home. On a month-to-month basis it is cheaper to write a rent check than a mortgage payment, which includes property tax and homeowner's insurance. But if you evaluate this scenario on a long-term basis, 20 years down the road the house has built equity, while the apartment gives you nothing in return. Although rent may be cheaper, it doesn't build equity.

The same can be said about term insurance. Term insurance is like renting, while cash value insurance is like owning since you build equity. If you are interested in recapturing your dollars you buy a house, you don't rent one. If you would like to recapture the dollars you paid in premiums for insurance, own it, don't rent it.

Let's take a look at 46 year old male, who is in good health and doesn't smoke. He applies for $250,000.00 worth of term insurance with the understanding that, according to the television commercial he saw, it will be cheaper. Using a 10 year term for a select nonsmoker, the annual premium would be approximately $345.00. In 10 years when that term expires, he wants the same coverage of $250,000.00, but to buy another 10 year term policy the premium would be about $697.00 per year. This, of course, assumes that term rates didn't increase, and that between the ages of 46 and 56, he remained in good health.

At age 66, it he still wishes to maintain the $250,000.00 death benefit for another term of 10 years, the annual premium would be around $1,835.00. Again, we are assuming his health is the same as it was when he was 46, and insurance rates didn't go up. However, at older ages, maintaining select nonsmoker rates would become more difficult. With each 10 year term that passes, to maintain this coverage he would have to re-qualify medically, and be approved by the insurance company. It is not uncommon for someone to be denied coverage, or because of health reasons, be charged additional premiums.

He believes that his life expectancy is about 80 years old, so at 76 he purchased another 10 year term policy. Unfortunately, he dies just before his 81st birthday. His premium at age 76 could be $7,870.00 per year. Again, assuming that he was in the same health classification as when he was 46 years old. At 76, it is almost a certainty that the premiums would be higher than that due to health problems.

What did he spend during his lifetime to have $250,000.00 of life insurance? From age 46 to 56 he spent $3,450.00. From age 56 to 66, he spent another $6,975.00. From age 66 to 76 another $18,350.00.00 was spent on premiums. Finally, from age 76 to 80, the premiums paid came to $39,350.00.

Unintended Consequences:
The Transfers

Age when policy issued	Annual Premium for $250,000.00	Ten Year Cumulative Cost
46	$345.00	$3,450.00
56	$697.50	$6,9750.00
66	$1,835.00	$18,350.00
76	$7,870.00	$39,350.00
	TOTAL PREMIUMS PAID	**$68,125.00**

Had he been able to invest all those premiums on a monthly basis and averaged 7% rate of return, he would have accumulated another $65,138.00 in opportunity costs. So, the actual cost of this term insurance including the lost opportunity cost would be . . .

$ 68,125.00   PREMIUM
$ 65,138.00   LOST OPPORTUNITY COSTS
$133,263.00

. . .a lot!!! Remember, that is assuming he had perfect health his entire life and insurance premiums didn't increase. That's a lot to assume.

TERM vs. CASH VALUE

Let's take the same 46 year old guy, buying one of the most expensive whole life policies he could buy. The annual premium for $250,000.00 of death benefit is in the neighborhood of $5,718.00 per year.[20] GULP! Remember, I wanted to use one of the most expensive policies I could find for this comparison. The $345.00 term premium for a 46 year old is far more attractive than $5,718.00 per year. However, in the whole life policy, the premium does not increase even though your health may change. Also, the whole life policy also builds up equity, or cash value. Under current values (values subject to change), at age 65, he would have paid $108,642.00 in premiums (19 years at $5,718.00), but the cash values built inside the policy are sufficient to continue to pay policy premiums for the rest of his life. Also, even as the premiums at age 65 are being paid by the policy, the cash value <u>continues</u> to grow.

If we compared just the base premiums of these two policies you could assume that the term insurance is a better buy.

$108,642	CASH VALUE PREMIUMS
$ 68,125	TERM PREMIUMS
$ 40,517	DIFFERENCE

But over this period of time, the cash value in the whole life policy has grown to $357,908.00 at age 81. One might come to the conclusion that paying an extra $40,517.00 in premiums over 35 years netted you $317,391.00 ($357,908.00 total cash value minus $40,517.00 difference in premiums). Remember also that the values in the cash

---

[20]Ohio National Life Insurance Company, Executive Estate Builder, December, 2002 Rates for 46 year old male, select nonsmoker on $250,000.00 death benefit.

value policy have grown tax-deferred and can be taken out of the policy tax-free by borrowing values or withdrawing the basis. Consider how much money you would have to have in a 401(k) to net $357,000.00 after taxes. Probably about $500,000. The whole life, cash value policy, financially, is a much better buy.

There is another major consideration. Remember, in our example, this guy died just before his 81st birthday. The term policy would have paid out **$250,000.00** to his beneficiaries. The whole life policy would have paid out **$485,000.00**. That's **$235,000.00** more tax-free dollars to the beneficiaries than the term policy would have paid out. Which policy was the better buy? At age 80, a **$485,000.00** death benefit in a term insurance policy would have an annual premium of **$43,500.00**.

IS IT OR ISN'T IT?

So, is term insurance cheaper over the entire lifetime of someone compared to cash value insurances? NO. Is term insurance cheaper for a short period of time? YES! Does term offer additional benefits other than the death benefit? NO. Can cash value policies be a financial tool? YES. Do investment people and insurance companies recommend term insurance? YES. Because it will be profitable to you? NO. Profitable to them? YES. There, see how easy that was?

POLICY SECRETS

Not everyone can afford $5,700.00 of annual premium. Whole life, cash value policies can be purchased for considerably less than what is used in my example. However, the lesson is: If you can recapture dollars you are spending for insurance, do it!

In whole life cash value policies, you have access to these cash values throughout your life. These values will grow tax deferred while the policy is in force. Access to cash values up to the premiums you paid into these policies can be withdrawn, surrendered or borrowed tax-free. Loans from the policies cash values are tax-free as long as interest is paid. Loans for business purposes in these policies are tax-free and the interest can be tax-deductible. Learning to use your life insurance policies can be beneficial, but BEWARE! Some "professionals" consider these policies easy pickings to surrender or strip the values out of them. BEWARE! IF AT ANY TIME, ANYONE RECOMMENDS THAT YOU DISCONTINUE A CASH VALUE POLICY, YOU MAY LOSE:

1. The immediate, income tax free death benefit protection under current law;
2. The loss of the tax deferral features;
3. The death benefit, which can assist in meeting IRS demands on your estate;
4. The flexibility of a personal source of loans at a low cost;
5. A wealth accumulator, tax planner, a conduit for money, a source of flexibility, security, and liquidity; and

6.   Future accumulation of your dollars because surrender charges could apply to your cash value.

A SECRET WEAPON

When used properly, these policies are very valuable tools.

- Under current tax laws, a cash value policy permits tax-deferred accumulation of money. Under current tax laws, the IRS will impose no tax on this policy unless you surrendered it or allow it to lapse. If you do so, they will tax the gains. The policy therefore can shelter you from taxes on any growth in the policy as long as it remains in effect.

- If your cash value has a waiver of premium and you become totally disabled by contract definition, the insurance company will make premium payments on your behalf to your contract. This will allow more freedom in how you use your discretionary funds for investment purposes.

- The cash in this policy is protected from creditors, absent fraudulent intent.

- This policy can help you fund your retirement by allowing you to spend your assets differently than if you retired without this insurance, assuming your insurance is in force at the time of retirement.

- Because this policy has a death benefit, in certain, limited circumstances, a reverse mortgage on your home may be used to create additional cash flow. You will be able to retain the house in your estate when you die through repayments to the bank using the death benefit.

- When you retire, you will not be confined to living on just some of the interest of your investments. The presence of this policy may allow you a great deal more freedom in the utilization of all of your other assets.

- You may, at a later age, use the death benefit as collateral for loans. Through leverage, the death benefit will be yours to spend. You can be a benefactor of your own policy. It is a unique piece of property.

- This policy will help in your estate planning to pass assets directly to your beneficiaries.

- This policy will develop cash for you in other ways. You will have a personal source from which you may borrow. Thus, on loans, you will save the interest, instead of sending those dollars off to a financial institution.

- Finally, don't forget what this policy can do for your family in the event of your death. They will be able to continue to live, and grow, and keep up with inflation, and retire just as you wish them to do were you alive.[21]

A SECRET BANK

As with the assets in your home, a cash value life insurance contract an be viewed as establishing another "bank" in your financial future. It could create financial options and opportunities when combined with other saving vehicles. It gives you liquidity, use and control of your money.

Let's say as an example, you did put $5,000.00 of annual premium into a cash value life insurance contract for 10 years. Your basis on this policy would be $50,000.00 ($5,000.00 x 10 years). During that 10 years, the equity had grown to $70,000.00 of cash value. You could withdraw $50,000.00 out of this policy (your basis) without creating a taxable event. This is so because the values are treated on a FIRST IN, FIRST OUT basis, thus the withdrawal of this $50,000.00 would be viewed as a return of basis and not taxable. However, if you requested the other $20,000 in the policy's values it would be taxed as ordinary income. You can avoid this tax by taking it out as a loan on the policy. The insurance company would you use your policy as collateral on this loan. Policy loans do not disrupt life insurances cash values. The insurance company lends you the money using your death benefit as

---

[21]Jerry LaValley, CLU, *The Power of Whole Life Insurance*, correspondence dated May 22, 2002.

collateral. Therefore, the cash values continue to grow regardless of the loan. Most companies offer very low net cost in borrowing against your cash values. Some contracts even have 0% net cost loans.

YOUR BANK, NOT THEIRS

Once again, gaining control of your money, is most important. Controlling the tax-free equity in your home, and establishing cash values inside life insurance policies to grow tax-deferred with favorable withdrawal and loan provisions, will be valuable financial tools for you. These two personal "banks" will help eliminate or reduce transfers of your wealth in the future. Eliminating or reducing transfers to others will save you an enormous amount of money that you are currently willing to give away. By using your "banks" you can eliminate or reduce fees, charges and interest that you are currently paying to others. By using your "banks," you can reduce the net costs of your loans, and in some cases deduct the interest or loans from your income tax. Remember, at your "bank," all the money you pay back goes back into your "bank" not theirs.

IT WAS TOO GOOD TO BE TRUE

Back in the 1980's, the government made an amazing change. In the midsts of eliminating almost all the tax deductions available to taxpayers, it also corralled another enemy of taxation: Cash value life insurance. The tax reform acts of the 1980's made it very clear that life insurance was a formidable foe of taxation. At that time private citizens, with no help from the government, could purchase life insurance, create cash values and escape a lot of taxation. The government was appalled. As the government has it's own savings programs, such as the IRA, they really didn't need or want any competition from the life insurance industry. You see, cash value life insurance policies were offering many more benefits than IRAs offer, so the government sought to control and limit life insurance policies. The public suffered the brunt of these government reforms, while the banks and investment companies applauded, since they were also direct beneficiaries of the regulation. For the government, it meant greater ways of taxing the public, and for the banks and investment companies, it meant a greater revenue flow.

ALL WAS NOT LOST

What the government set out to do was to limit the amount of money that a person could put into a life insurance policy. Cash value policies offer tax deferred accumulation of values and well-informed people at that time were putting as much money as they could into these policies. The tax reform acts of the 1980's did limit the amount of money that can be put into cash value life insurance. Lucky for us, what they failed to do was to reduce the benefits within the policies. The next time you consider opening an IRA or other investment account, consider whether it offers the any of the following benefits, which are inherent in many cash value policies:

- TAX-DEFERRED GROWTH. Outside of qualified plans, mutual funds, CD's, stocks and other investment products don't offer tax-deferred growth of your money.

- COMPARABLE RATES OF RETURN. Everyone advertises great rates but you must also take into consideration taxes, and whether you can maintain liquidity, use, and control of your money.

- GUARANTEES. Do mutual funds and stocks offer specific guarantees or are you exposed to losses?

- SAFETY. Can you sleep at night knowing your investments will be there when you need them?

- ACCESS. Can you get to your money or is it locked in place because of fees and/or penalties?

- CONTROL. Do you control the outcome of your investments or does someone else? When someone else controls your money it usually ends up costing you more!

- DISABILITY. If you become disabled, will your bank or investment people, on your behalf, continue to deposit money for you on a monthly basis because you physically and financially are unable to? Will they continue to make these monthly deposits until age 65? No.

- PROTECTION FROM CREDITORS. Will creditors, for the purpose of collecting debt, have access to your stocks, mutual funds, retirement plans, bank accounts, and CD's? Yes.

- TAX-FREE WITHDRAWALS. Do your retirement plans, stocks, CD's, and/or mutual funds offer tax-free withdrawals or will you have to pay fees, penalties, taxes, or all three to get your money?

- PROBATE. Do your retirement plans, stocks, mutual funds, real estate, bank savings, CD's, and other savings programs, in the event of your death end up in probate court?

- INSURED. Are your stocks and mutual funds insured for failure?

- DEATH BENEFIT. Do your mutual funds, CD's, or stocks give your family sums of tax-free money upon your death?

- SELF-COMPLETING. Are any of your investments self-completing? This means if your intention of saving and investing money was projected over a 30 year period, and you die after only 5 years, your family would still receive the other 25 years of investments and earnings that had been planned on, tax-free? Would the banks, government, or investment people do that for you?

The features listed about are some of the benefits that escaped the legislation of the 1980's that remain benefits in cash value life insurance.

Unintended Consequences:
The Transfers

THE CORRIDOR

Who determines the cost of term insurance? The insurance companies. Who determines the cost of cash value insurance? The government, by regulation.

Cash value insurance	Government regulated

THE CORRIDOR

Term insurance	Industry regulated

The government regulates and limits the amount of money you can put into these policies. If you put more money into a cash value policy than government regulations allow, it becomes a modified endowment contract and would be treated and taxed as qualified plans are treated and taxed. We can deduce that a maximized cash value policy, with its tax advantages, is the best policy you are allowed to have by law.

QUALIFIED PLANS

Cash value insurance	Government regulated
Tax-Deferred Growth	Avoids Probate
Competitive Rate of Return	Insured
Safety	Some Guarantees
Access to Your Money	Tax Free Death Benefit
Control	Tax Free Withdrawals
Disability Features	Protection from Creditors

Term insurance	Industry regulated

Unintended Consequences:
The Transfers

Looking at all the benefits listed in the diagrams above, would you agree that cash value life insurance would be a good place to park at least some of your money? Learning how to use this vehicle during your life can become a very valuable financial tool. By regulating it, it's obvious that the government sees it as a valuable financial tool, why don't you?

WHY YOU BUY

As you can see, much time can be spent talking about life insurance. What it really breaks down to is this: Need vs. Want. While you're alive you want your family to have the best that your lifestyle will allow. The best home, the best car, the best education, etc. What about if you die? Do you want your family now to get by on simply what they need, a small home, a run down car, and no money for the kids' education? Is that the commitment you made to your family? The question is, WHAT DO YOU REALLY WANT TO HAPPEN IF YOU'RE NOT THERE?

TRANSFER 7:

DISABILITY
THE SUPREME WEALTH TRANSFER

One of the most unfortunate losses in life is one's ability to earn a living. Think of it. . . you're earning a good living, paying your bills and taxes, and living a very comfortable lifestyle, and in one moment you lose the ability to pay for all of it. How long can you live on your savings before they are depleted? How long can you maintain your standard of living? Maybe three or four months? Then what?

If you have an asset, in many cases it is insured. It's compulsory to have automobile insurance in the event of a serious accident. You insure your homes for fire, theft, and other casualties. These assets can be replaced when properly insured. If you are disabled and your ability to earn money is lost, what then? Can this happen to you? Each year, one in eight people are disabled.[22] Chances of a 30 year old becoming disabled for more than three months before the age of 65 is 54%.[23] For someone 50 years old, the chances of becoming disabled before the age of 65 is 33%.[24] The odds of you becoming disabled are two and a half times higher than the odds of your

---

[22]Society of Actuaries, 1985.

[23]*Id.*

[24]*Id.*

premature death.[25] The average duration of a disability over 90 days for a 30 year old is 2.5 years and for a 50 year old it is 3.1 years.[26]

If you have an annual income of $36,000.00 and you save 10% a year, it will take you 25 years at 5% interest to save 5 years of your net income. So who will pay the bills? Maybe you could borrow the money you need. Don't bother going to the bank. They will look at you as someone who has no ability, no income, to repay the loan. How about from relatives or friends? This kind of charity has its limits. Maybe your spouse, if you have one, can get a second job. Perhaps you will have to sell off some of your assets. In most cases though the forced sale of an asset generally means reduced value of that asset.

GUARANTEEING A SECURE FUTURE?

Well, you could always apply for Social Security disability benefits. Although, to qualify for these benefits, first you must satisfy a five month waiting period, and be unable to do any job. You must have the type of disability that will likely last more than one year in length or result in death.

You also may believe your income is protected by worker's compensation coverage. However, worker's compensation is only available if you are injured or

---

[25]*Id.*

[26]*Id.*

disabled while on the job. If you work 8 hours a day, who covers the other 16 hours of the day? What about weekends, vacations, sporting injuries, car accidents, or major illnesses?

It is possible that through your employment you may be covered under a group disability policy. If you are, it is important to know when the benefit begins, the definition of what constitutes a disability, how much you are entitled to receive, and for how long. Many group policies are limited in their coverage. Also, if you leave your employer, it is unlikely that you'll be able to continue the coverage. In the event of a disability, none of these sources will guarantee a secure future.

THE GOOSE OR THE GOLDEN EGGS?

If you owned the proverbial goose that was laying golden eggs, would you insure the goose or the eggs? Obviously you would want to insure both, but losing the goose would be much worse than losing an egg or two. The goose represents the future, the ability to create more eggs. Without that ability, well, your goose is cooked. You would have to find a way to replace that flow of eggs you became accustomed to. Don't look at me, I don't lay eggs just for anyone.

You can insure your income by purchasing a disability income policy. There are a limited number of companies that sell this coverage. The strength of the coverage will be based on the definitions of coverage in the policy. The premiums of these policies will vary. The more coverage and benefits, the higher the premium. The coverage should be for <u>your</u> occupation, not <u>any</u> occupation. This means, if you're a dentist and become disabled, you could get a job at the Dairy Queen and still receive disability for your former occupation, being a dentist. Some policies would halt benefits for this disability because of your ability to perform any job, regardless of what it was.

Your income is your most valuable asset. Without it you're in deep trouble. You can spend your entire life building your fortune, and lose it in one second. Accidents, illnesses, stress-related impairments, cancer, heart attack, and stroke can disrupt and affect your total financial picture. Forty-nine percent of all home foreclosures are due to disability. Don't leave yourself and your family exposed in the event of disability. Relying on luck, or dumb luck, is not the solution.

TRANSFER 8:

<u>FINANCING</u>
<u>AUTOMOBILES</u>

DRIVING YOU CRAZY?

As I discussed earlier, most of the things we purchase in life are depreciating assets. Next to your home, the automobile is one of the most expensive transfers of your wealth you can make. Unlike your home, a car does not retain its value. Also, most auto purchases are financed. You must pay back not only the principal, but also the interest. But unlike your home mortgage payments, the interest is not tax-deductible. For the purchase of a $30,000.00 car, at 6% interest for five years, your payment would be $579.98 per month. You will be transferring away $4,799.00 of interest to the bank. Their bank, not yours. Once again, like the purchase of your home, the focus is on what auto payment you think you can afford each month, not the transfers you are making.

I would like to share with you the actual cost of owning cars in one's lifetime. Let's say you are 35 years old. You want to buy a new car about every four years. You estimate you will probably drive until you are 79 years old, and at that age probably very slowly. You also believe you can average about 7% rates of return during that time. You also figure the cars will cost about $30,000.00 each. I've added a 4% inflation factor into the cost of the cars and sales tax. I'm using 6% loan interest rate.

During your lifetime you will have purchased 10 cars. If you had been able to invest just the interest at 7%, you would have accumulated $576,473.00 by the time you were 79. After all, those years of driving, all you really end up with is one 4 year old used car worth about $20,000.00.

What makes this transfer of your wealth painful, is that the interest paid to their banks is not tax-deductible. If you could find a lending institution that would allow you to deduct that interest from your taxes, would you be interested in giving that institution your business?

YOU CAN DO THIS

Throughout this book, I have encouraged you to begin to establish your own "banks." One of these "banks" is centered around the equity in your home. By establishing your home equity line of credit "bank," you can use it to make purchases and most likely deduct the interest paid on that purchase. Purchasing your car using your equity line of credit "bank" could be an excellent option to recapture transferred interest.

If you were to purchase a car for $30,000.00, the note from the bank or lending institution is designed to cover the full value of the car plus interest over the period of the note. A car is a depreciating asset. It loses value every year you own it. Why would you want to pay this loan off as fast as you can? After all, once it is paid for, all it can do is lose value. If you insist on losing your money from this type of transfer, that is unfortunate.

However, after a car auto is paid off, it still has some value, resale value. Think about this, take your time and then think some more: Why would you want to pay this car off beyond its residual or resale value? To please some bankers or finance company? That may be their goal in life but it is not mine. If I know approximately what the resale value, residual, or blue book price of my car will be in 4 years, I only want to pay my car down to that amount. Even if the car's value in 4 years is only $6,000.00, why should you continue to make $500.00 monthly payments on something that will lose another $2,000.00 in value in a year?

If you could adjust your monthly payments to bring the balance of your loan to the resale value of your car, you should do it. In this scenario, your monthly car payment would be reduced from $500.00 to $250.00 per month. Now, you can't make these adjustments using a traditional bank or lending institution, but you can if you use your "bank." Remember, using your "bank," the interest you pay on this loan may also be deductible.

If you were able to save $250.00 per month from your car payment for even just one year, at 6% interest you would have saved $3,099.31. Remember, your car's value didn't go up because you paid it off early. It will only go down. You create a large lost opportunity cost by paying off a depreciating asset early.

By purchasing your car using your equity line of credit, you can adjust your monthly payments on this loan. In the first couple of years on this loan, you would pay back to your "bank" exactly what the payment would have been if you had used traditional financing. You were going to make this payment to a finance company anyway, now you're paying it to yourself. As the years go by you can find out what the residual or resale value of your car will be. Then, you can adjust your monthly payment so the loan balance doesn't go below the residual or resale value of your car. If you sell the car, you pay off the loan to "your bank" with the proceeds, and follow the same procedure to purchase your next car. If you trade the car in, the balance of your new car should be reduced by the value of your trade-in. You can then borrow from "bank" the balance due after the trade-in. If you purchased another $30,000.00 car, your trade in of $4,000.00 is equal to your "bank's" loan balance. You know you still owe the $4,000.00 to your "bank" on the old car, but the loan amount needed on the new car is $26,000.00 not $30,000.00 because of your trade-in. To be safe, you should reduce by 20% any residual or resale value of your car in calculating any adjustment of your monthly payment. Remember, equity line of credit loan rates are adjustable, and are not a long-term fixed rate. Your interest rates could go up. That's reality. The rates could also go down. That's hoping. If rates went up you have the option of going to "their bank" to shop their current fixed rate loans to refinance this debt. Traditionally though, equity line of credit rates have been lower than car loan rates.

REAL LIFE EXAMPLE

I met with a client who recently established an equity line of credit. He had just traded in his old car for a new one. After the trade-in, the balance of the new car was $13,500.00. He borrowed the money from his equity line of credit "bank." The minimum payment to his equity loan was $55 per month for the car. He was paying $300 a month back to his bank. In about 4 years, the car would be paid off, and he took a tax deduction for the interest paid on this loan.

I told him he was doing a great job, but that we should dig a one layer deeper in this thought process. I said, "Let's call the dealership where you bought the car and ask them what the residual price of the car would be in 4 years." We did, and the salesman said the residual would be about $6,000.00 in 4 years. The car's original price was $20,000.00. I said, "Let's reduce that residual by 20% just to be on the safe side." That came to $4,800.00. I looked at him and asked, "Do you recognize the opportunity that is in front of you? If you pay $150.00 per month on your car loan, in 4 years the balance will be $4,400.00 on the loan from your bank. The adjusted residual value of your car will be $4,800.00. If you sell the car, you can pay off your loan. If you trade in your car it will reduce the purchase price. But, by reducing your payment from $300.00 to $150.00, you can save $150.00 per month for 4 years, and at 7% you could accumulate $8,329.00. Additionally, you will also benefit from about $400.00 in tax savings." I asked him again, "Now, do you see the opportunity before you?"

It is so important to recapture your dollars. You can see that people transfer away, unknowingly and unnecessarily, so much money its mind boggling. It's time to take a stand, but you can't until you have the knowledge to do so. Lets face it, no one in the financial world, is going out of their way to teach you the efficiency of money. What is important to understand is not what you pay for an auto, but <u>how</u> you pay for it.

TRANSFER 9:

CREDIT CARDS

Credit cards have become part of the American culture. The marketing and advertising for these cards almost make you feel dumb for not using them. Well, someone's mama once said, "Stupid is as stupid does." The credit card is often misused and misunderstood. Most 18 year olds are bombarded by these card companies. The, "I want it now generation," usually subscribes to four or five credit cards. Unfortunately, they purchase everything on credit. Where did they learn these financial tactics? You can start at home.

When I was a kid and a little rebellious, I would show my parents how grown up I was by growing my hair a little long and staying out 20 minutes past my curfew. I showed them! Today, kids prove they are grown up by showing their parents they don't need them financially. (As a side note, they will still live at home, eat all your food, and leave all the lights on when they disappear with their friends. They also have no problem feeding their friends before they leave.) Some parents are overjoyed that their kid is finally buying their own stuff. That joy dissolves after receiving those 8 a.m. phone calls everyday from credit card collectors. The kid doesn't see the problem, because he just got a letter in the mail from the credit card company increasing his credit limit. This is the parents' purgatory for not teaching their kids anything about money.

Today, on average, consumers are carrying a record amount of debt. Bankruptcies are at record highs and increasing every year. Personal debt in the United States can and will ruin the economy if it is not addressed. The financial future of our country will be altered severely if the next generation is so laden with debt, from college loans to credit card debt, that they will never get out of their financial hole. Their bad credit ratings will follow them for years, stifling major purchases they wish or need to make. As a whole, it will affect our economy. Of course, if they need to make purchases in the future, they will have to pay higher interest rates. Remember, this is the future generation that we hope (the older folks) will also pay for all our future government and social benefits. There will also be less of them than there are us, so in many ways this is a serious problem.

Baby boomers, the keep-up-with-the-Joneses generation, are the biggest offenders. They think nothing of carrying four to five thousand dollar balances on their credit cards. This is a serious transfer of your wealth. If you have a credit card balance of $5,000.00 at 18% , you will pay $39,433.00 in interest over a 40 year period. That interest, had you been able to invest at 8% over 40 years, would have earned you $255,383.00. If your credit card company is getting 18% on their investments, the interest you paid them over that 40 year period would net them $6,680,280.00. That's just on one account. If you have any dream of growing and maintaining your wealth, you must avoid the credit card trap. The obvious solution would be to restrict the use of your credit cards.

YOU CAN BANK ON IT

If you have established your "banks," the solution to this credit card problem is clearer. An equity line of credit "bank" would do the trick. If you have $5,000.00 of credit card debt at 18%, how would you like to lower the interest rate to 5% or 6% and deduct the interest from your taxes? How would you also like to lower the monthly payment on this debt from $200.00 per month to $100.00? By paying off the credit card debt with your "bank," you will make payments back to yourself at one-third of the interest rate. It is IMPORTANT to remember that you have only shifted this debt, not paid it off. Once again, though you have become more efficient with your money, you have taken a bad debt situation and made it more tolerable. You also reduced your monthly expense for debt by $100.00. That money could be better used elsewhere.

Just about anything is better than paying 14%, 16%, or 18% interest rates. If you had established a cash value life insurance contract, the values inside of this contract can be withdrawn or borrowed. If borrowed, the loan rates on these policies would be considerably lower then the credit card rate. Somewhere in the range of 6% to 7%. This would reduce your monthly payment on the credit card debt. But remember our previous discussion. Some life insurance companies will credit interest on the loaned amount even though you have taken the money out of the policy. This would make the net loan rate interest about one to two percent. Also, the loan from the policy is tax-free, however the interest from the policy loan is NOT tax deductible.

Again, always pay back the loans from your

"banks." You will use them over and over in the future. Pay off credit card balances monthly if you can. Know your budget limits. Huge credit card balances usually indicate a lack of financial discipline. A credit card can be your best friend and your worst nightmare. Use it wisely. You'll sleep better at night.

TRANSFER 10:

<u>INVESTMENTS</u>

Any dollars that you are able to recapture, that you were unknowingly and unnecessarily giving away, can either be saved to one of your "banks" or used to enhance your lifestyle. By eliminating or reducing these transfers, the monthly amount of money you will be able to keep will increase.

When investing and accumulating money there is more than meets the eye. If a 35 year old married couple was able to save $5,000.00 per year for 30 years assuming a 7% rate of return, they would accumulate $543,426.00 by age 65. That's a large sum of money. They could conclude that they spent $155,000.00 ($5,000.00 times 30 years plus $5,000.00) to accumulate $543,426.00. It could be said that the $155,000.00 they saved netted them $388,426.00 after deposits ($543,426.00 - $155,000.00 = $388,426.00). This amount represents the interest they earned. In my example, they will be paying the taxes due on this accumulation right from the investment account. Over that 30 year period, there will be $155,371.00 in taxes due.

$543,426.00   Accumulated
-$155,371.00 Taxes
<u>-$155,000.00</u> Invested
$233,056.00   Balance less expenses

Most investors let their investment compound through re-investment. Normally, in that situation, they get the money to pay the taxes due from their lifestyle. At some point, their standard of living will suffer from the payment of taxes due annually on this account. Also, at some point in time, the annual tax due every year will be greater than their annual deposit. In the example I am using, in the 17th year, the tax due on this account ($5,202.00) will be more than their annual deposit of $5,000.00. If you pay a tax you could have avoided, not only do they lose that money but also the money they could have earned from that money. That is known as lost opportunity cost. If they paid $155,371.00 in taxes, they also lost the ability to earn $142,323.00 from those tax payments. Now, lets take a look:

$543,426.00	Accumulated
-$155,000.00	Invested
-$155,371.00	Taxes
-$142,323.00	Opportunity cost on tax
$ 90,733.00	Total minus costs

If they could have avoided or reduced the tax on this account they would have saved hundreds of thousands of dollars. You could now say they spent $155,000.00 over 30 years to net $90,733.00. Even though this was calculated at a 7% rate of return, the net rate of return is actually 2.97%. Do people pay more taxes than they have to? Yes, but not because they want to.

THE CREATORS
OF THE
TRANSFERS

THE GOVERNMENT:
YOUR PARTNER IN LIFE AND DEATH

God created morons, he also created politicians. I'm sorry, I've repeated myself. The passion of politicians, and the harm that they cause, leads me to wonder why more of them don't commit suicide. We have invented the government of compromise. For the past 100 years or so, the government has passed on compromised solutions to our problems. Years later even the compromises are compromised. This, over a period of time, waters down the original solution, thus creating loopholes in the law that now need new compromises to close up the loopholes. If the Ten Commandments had been compromised over the years in this fashion, you would end up with the rules for big time wrestling.

In my opinion, there is greater disdain for the government and its failures by the public in general than ever before. Two monolithic political parties bent on destroying each other and willing to use the public as pawns, fight for ultimate control and power. Their goal is to fulfill their agenda, not the public's. I am tempted to run for president in the next election, independently of course, under the name of Mr. Neither. Mr. I. M. Neither. I bet the votes would flow in. I believe that NONE OF THE ABOVE should also be a choice for voters. This would give politicians time to reflect just how disconnected from reality politicians can get.

Other than what I stated above, I believe our form of government is almost perfect. Remember, our country's decisions are being made by a small minority of the population. Only 50% of eligible voters vote, and the winners of the election average 53% of the votes by 50% of the voters, thus about 26% of the public voted for the winner. When you take into account the people who never registered to vote, the winning politicians move to Washington with only about 15% of the people believing in him. Soon all that may be left are compromised fragments of a once promising, powerful society.

SOMETHING FOR NOTHING

Every time the government concedes to do something, it costs you money. No matter how impractical or how generous government programs sound, they are expensive. With the proper amount of media exposure and a loud special interest group, a politician would promote a hog-calling contest in Alaska at your expense. This is a government that believes it can produce medical benefit coverage for elderly people for about $50.00 per month. The going rate for that coverage in the private sector is about $500.00 per month. They continue to foolishly and recklessly spend money and create more debt. Here is just a few of the bargains we're getting for our money, from Martin L. Gross' book, <u>The Government Racket 2000 and Beyond</u>:

- *A $1,000,000 study on how to cross the street in Utah*
- *$90,000 to study the social life of vegetarians*
- *Millions to fund over 150 government owned golf courses*
- *Hundreds of thousands of dollars to fund the*

Unintended Consequences:
The Creators of the Transfers

National First Ladies Library
- *Over $200,000 to study horseflies' sex lives*
- *Over $20 million to study mail delivery*
- *Over $25 million for political conventions*
- *Over $20,000 for 3 elevator floors in congress*
- *Over $300,000 for a barber shop and beauty salon in congress*
- *Over $200,000 on a study why women smile more than men*
- *Over $100,000 for the plans to design an outhouse in Delaware. (Over $300,000 to build it.)*
- *$4 million for a parking lot in Illinois*
- *$40 million for the National Animal Disease Center in Ames, Iowa*
- *$400,000 for manure management research at the National Swine Research Center*
- *$800,000 for a project on red imported fire ants*
- *$880,000 for cotton research in Texas*
- *$5,670,000 for wood utilization research*
- *$484,000 University of Connecticut for Food Marketing Policy Center*
- *$260,000 for asparagus technology in Washington*
- *$239,000 for fruit practices in Michigan*
- *$1 million for University of Alaska Stellar Sea Lion recovery*
- *$750,000 to prevent Atlantic salmon from escaping state stream in Alaska*
- *$250,000 to prepare discussions regarding Columbia River's hydro system in Alaska*
- *$3,350,000 for the Institute of Politics in New Hampshire*
- *$3 million for Hawaiian Sea Turtles*

Unintended Consequences:
The Creators of the Transfers

- *$300,000 to develop a virtual business incubator at Lewis and Clark College*
- *$50,000 for a tattoo removal program in California*
- *$15 million for financial aid at the Citadel in South Carolina*
- *$1 million for math teacher leadership*
- *$750,000 for minority aviation training at William Lehman Aviation Center (this money goes to only 12 students, making Florida Memorial College more expensive than Harvard or Yale)*
- *$2 million for the House of Food and Friends (This program is being run by a convicted criminal who had previously stolen money from another charity)*
- *$5 million for computer equipment and internet access for schools in Armenia*
- *$1 million for the Conflict Transformation Across Cultures program at the school of International Training. Problem is only 40 students per year participate making this a $25,000 per student subsidy.* [27]

Thousands of these government giveaways happen every year. These drive up the country's debt, which you and I are responsible for paying. Ironically, the politicians want tell us what we should be doing financially. The real problem is every time you try to financially help yourself

---

[27]Gross, Martin L., <u>The Government Racket 2000 and Beyond.</u> New York: Harper-Collins Publishers, Inc., 2000.

and your family, you're taxed. If we followed their model of fiscal responsibility, the country would collapse economically. Historically, we saw the fall of the U.S.S.R. due in part to the cost of the "Cold War." Their debt buried them. I fear our country's debt, compounded by personal debt, leaves very little wiggle room for the government to do the things they are promising to do. The problem is compounded by the future demographics of our country. With individuals carrying record amounts of debt, politicians feel they maybe committing political suicide by adding more debt to the public in the form of tax increases.

FINANCIALLY SPEAKING

The reason I have brought all this up is this: The largest financial transfers of your wealth are created by the government in the form of taxes. Their actions will affect your money more than anything else in your entire life. The real bad news is they can make up the rules as they go along. There is an interesting debate simmering. Is the money we earn ours, or does it belong to the government and we are just using it? Think about it. The uncertainty of taxation rates in the future continues to be a problem. The growing aging population problem, over-spending, growing debt, increased costs of health care, the never ending war on terror, increased spending on security, will all affect the amount of money that you will be able to keep and spend in the future.

Qualified retirement savings plans could become a bigger tax revenue target in the future. Just understanding that this could happen and searching out alternative savings for retirement could save you thousands of tax dollars in the future. The government has a vested interest in all the money you are saving. They are taking it seriously. You should too.

THE BANKS

It is truly reassuring and comforting to know that your bank savings, should the bank fail, is insured by an agency of our federal government that is over $6 trillion dollars in debt itself. Someone once said, "Banks will lend you money if you can prove to them you don't need it. A banker is a fellow who lends you his umbrella when the sun is shining and wants it back the minute it begins to rain."

NEVER GO INTO A BANK WITHOUT A TEN FOOT POLE

Let's get one thing straight here. You, by putting money into a bank, are lending money to that bank, so they can lend it to someone else. They earn interest from that loan and charge fees to it on a regular basis. In return for you "lending" the money to the bank, you receive a pitiful interest rate, but they also charge you fees to keep that account open at their bank. Think about it. . . you put the money in their savings account and receive 2% earnings. You may also be charged fees for that savings account. They take your money and lend it to someone in the form of a credit card and receive 18% interest and receive fees on a monthly basis for that credit card.

Not only do they charge us interest, but they charge fees. They raise existing fees, invent new ones and make it harder to avoid them by raising minimum balance requirements. Looking through my bank records and the documents given to me when I opened my accounts, I found and identified over one hundred separate fees banks impose on their customers. Over the past few years the size of the fees rose twice the rate of inflation. Charges and fees account for more than 40% of the banks revenues. The banks have become a fee-based operation. They consider you naive when it comes to the sophisticated business of banking. They determine there are certain things you don't "need to know." Here is a partial list of fees and charges I found:

Saving account fee	*Check cashing fee*
Monthly account fee	*Automated transaction fee*
Manual transaction fee	*Monthly overdraft mgmt. fee*
Automatic payment amend fee	*VISA account fee*
Withdrawal fee	*Automatic payment fee*
Set up fee	*Unpaid bill payment fee*
Checking account fee	*Account special request fee*
Checking overnight fee	*Stop payment checking fee*
Checking account statement fee	*Dishonor fee*
Customer investigation fee	*Overdraft application fee*
Online banking fee	*ATM fees*
International service fee	*Traveler's checks fees*
Bank draft fee	*International money transfers fee*
Safe deposit fee	*Home loan application fee*
Personal loan fee	*Credit card replacement fee*
Credit card collection fee	*Cash advance fee*
Telephone call center fee	*Account closure fee*
Wire transfer fee	*Garnishment fee*
Notary fee	*Levies*
Special statement cutoff fee	*Telephone transfer fee*
Night deposit fee	*Analyzed business fee*
Loan processing fee	*Tax service fee*
Appraisal fee	*Credit report fee*
Survey fee	*Closing title company fee*
Recording fee	*Escrow waiver fee*

Unintended Consequences:
The Creators of the Transfers

Inspection fee
Courier fee
Attorney fee
Early payoff fee

Underwriting fee
Document prep fee
Late payment fee

You would think the government would step in and help protect its citizens. That's what they are paid to do right? WRONG! You see, the government needs the banks. The Federal Reserve, which represents banks in this country, prints our dollars and lends them to the Federal government, which in turn creates the ever-growing federal debt. The government pays interest on these loans. This debt is passed on to you and me in the form of taxation. If this debt continues to grow will <u>your</u> taxes ever go down? No. Who is happy with this whole scenario? Yes, the banks. They charge interest on that debt. It costs the banks very little to print the money to give to the government. It costs the government very little to dole out this money. However, we will spend our entire lives paying on this debt in the form of taxes, without ever coming <u>close</u> to paying it off completely. That is why you will never see the government aggressively go after the banks. They need each other!

The government will willingly pay off large loans that defaulted, to the banks, in order to keep them solvent. Large loans to third world countries are written off every year by the banks only to have the government bail them out. Loans to companies that create political favor, are approved with a nod and a wink. You and I are left with the tab. When it comes to your wealth neither the banks or the government care about your best interest.

ENOUGH IS ENOUGH

Elderly people will be grilled by bank employees when trying to withdraw large sums of money. They will be asked what they intend to do with it. The banks will use scare tactics to imply that what the clients are planning to do with the money is crazy or ill-advised. In reality, it's none of their business what someone wants to do with their money. The bank's aim is to hold your money as long as they possible can, since for every day they hold it is one more day of earnings to be made from your money.

Also, getting financial information and advice from a bank can be a huge mistake. Their focus is to control your money and collect interest and charge fees WHENEVER they can. They will steer you to their bank products when it comes to investments and saving, not because those products are the best choice for you, but because they profit from sales of their products. Also, the financial consultants housed in banks cannot sell other company's investments or products, even if another company's product is better suited for you and your financial profile. But they don't tell you that they merely give you the idea that their bank's products are the best for you. The less informed you are the better bank client you become. No one is safe. If you need "banking service" (that is an oxymoron, by the way), find yourself a local credit union. It is the lesser of two evils.

As discussed in previous chapters the ideal solution would be to create your own "banks." Follow the rules of basic banking. Learn to pay your banks back, save the interest and whenever possible, deduct interest payments when the law allows. Your "banks" will be funded by eliminating or reducing the ten major transfers of your wealth. The savings could be staggering.

THE FEDERAL RESERVE:

BRIDGING THE GAP TO PLUNDER

The central core of banking under the guide of the Federal Reserve is very simple: An ability to print money at very little cost, which has no real value, no backing of gold or silver, and loan it out to purchase things that do have value. This in return provides value to the unbacked money printed. Holding property liens on things you purchased, gives the banks the right to book these as bank assets, minus the balance of the debt. All the money that has been created by the banks is created out of nothing.

In November, 1910, a secret meeting was held on Jekyll Island in Georgia.[28] Present at this meeting were Senator Nelson Aldrich, Chairman of the National Monetary Commission, associate of JP Morgan, father-in-law to John D. Rockefeller Jr. Also present were: Abraham Pratt Andrew, Assistant secretary of the U.S. Treasury; Frank A. Vanderlip, President of the National City Bank of New York, representing William Rockefeller and the international banking house of Kuhn, Loeb, and Company; Henry P. Davison, Senior partner of JP Morgan Company; Charles D. Norton, President of JP Morgan's First National Bank of New York; Benjamin Strong, head of JP Morgan's Bankers Trust Company, and; Paul M.

---

[28]G. Edward Griffin, <u>The Creature from Jekyll Island</u>. California: American Media, 1994.

Warburg, partner in Kuhn, Loeb, and Company, a representative of the Rothschild banking dynasty in England and France, brother to Max Warburg, head of the Warburg banking consortium in Germany and the Netherlands.[29]

Every one of the participants were pledged to secrecy. It was only after many years and much research that the meeting and its purpose was uncovered. What formed out of this meeting was a banking cartel, a proposed monopoly of the industry. By doing this they would create control of the financial monetary systems, yours, mine, and the government's. Even creating a name for this cartel was well thought out. They agreed that the word "bank" should not be used in its title. Thus, the birth of the Federal Reserve, a cartel agreement with five objectives:

1) Stop the growing competition from the nations newer banks;

2) Obtain a franchise to create money out of nothing for the purpose of lending;

3) Get control of the reserves of all banks so that the more reckless ones would not be exposed to currency drains and banks runs;

4) Get the taxpayers to pick up the cartel's inevitable losses, and;

5) Convince Congress that the purpose was to protect the public.[30]

---

[29]*Id.*

[30]*Id.*

Specifically, the Federal Reserve was designed as legal private monopoly of the money supply, operated for the benefit of the monopolists under the guise of protecting and promoting the public welfare.

Constitutional restraints prohibited the federal government from printing paper fiat money.[31] Fiat money is money that have no valuable asset, gold, silver, etc., to back it. However, there is no such restraint on the Federal Reserve. But, the banks, i. e. the Federal Reserve, wanted the government to have a system to pay for the money they printed for the government. Say the magic words: Sixteenth Amendment. This amendment allowed the government to charge a tax on income.[32] At that time, the federal gold and silver reserves were still efficient enough to back all its printed money. As the country continued to grow and the advent of government social spending increased, the government surpassed the ability to back its fiat money. In its own wisdom, the government eliminated its gold and silver standards. Remember the days when our printed money stated that it was a silver certificate right on the front of the bill? That's gone. So are our gold and silver stockpiles. Now the printed money says "Federal Reserve Note" across the top. Since that change, the national debt (not the deficit, they are two different things) has spiraled out of control. Our country's debt is

---

[31]United States Constitution, 10th Amendment.

[32]United States Constitution, 16th Amendment.

compounded because the Federal Reserve charges interest on that debt, which is repaid by the tax revenues collected by the government.

The connection between the banks and the government is an interesting one. I would recommend the reading of the book <u>The Creature From Jekyll Island</u> by G. Edward Griffin. It is an in-depth look at the Federal Reserve.

Understanding how the government, banks, and Federal Reserve relate to each other will open your eyes to the transfers of your wealth that they have created, controlled, and profited from. Remember, they are the ones constantly reminding us that they will help us financially. The reality is, between the three of them, we transfer away over two-thirds of our wealth over our lifetimes. All the plans and products they support create unintended consequences for us and more profits for them.

MISGUIDED
WISDOM

FUZZY WUZZY THINKING

It has been long since I've seen an investment broker, accountant, or talk show financial experts prove mathematically that any of their opinions work. I'm not talking about the one-sided comparison where they blow off any idea contrary to theirs as stupid. (Meaning, if you don't do it their way, you must be lacking intellectually.) By disarming those who even dare to think outside their box as "stupid," these self-proclaimed experts don't have to prove a thing. People, in general, take offense to being called stupid, so they tend to take the their-opinion-must-be-fact of these experts as gospel, fearing the wrath of being labeled.

Imagine being confronted by two salesmen selling laundry detergent. The first salesman says, "Well, you would be stupid to buy a detergent that doesn't create enough suds to clean." The other salesman says, "You're stupid if you believe what the first guy said." Great comparison, eh? No matter what you do, you're stupid by someone's account. I have heard professionals in the financial industry tell clients essentially the same thing. "You would have to be dumb to pass this up." "It wouldn't take a rocket scientist to figure this out." "How long do you want to be ripped off?" There are hundreds of statements like these made everyday implying that you're stupid.

I was watching one of these so-called financial expert's TV show, we'll call her Ms. Fuzzy, and I was amazed how many times she implied the callers were stupid. She did it in a nice way, but the implication was that the caller was stupid, and she wasn't. Ninety percent of what she told people was simply her opinion, NOT fact. To be an expert, Ms. Fuzzy knows she must deal with lower intellects to maintain her lofty title of "expert." But when cornered, Ms. Fuzzy reverts to belittling the caller rather than give the caller a legitimate answer. Then she dismisses the caller's ideas as "dumb" and frowns at the television audience to emphasize the point.

Ms. Fuzzy received a call from someone who bought life insurance, the "wrong kind," according to Ms. Fuzzy. Her conclusion went something like this, "Get rid of that and the guy that sold it to you." (You're stupid.) "He is a salesman" (You're really stupid.) "A S-A-L-E-S-M-A-N, that's all!" (You have moved from the stupid class to the idiots class.) Great reasoning, Ms. Fuzzy! Nice comparison, filled with knowledge and facts. One question for you Ms. Fuzzy: Is it salesmen that you hate? Probably just about everything Ms. Fuzzy owns, she purchased from a S-A-L-E-S-M-A-N. Does that make her stupid?

To come to her conclusions for this caller, Ms. Fuzzy used no math, no facts, no research, no independent studies. There was no discussion about income, cost, age, family status, amount of insurance, the person's personal debt, their tax bracket, the love of his family, or quality of the company. NOTHING, NOTHING, NOTHING to justify her "conclusion," just Ms. Fuzzy's opinion. How one can have such a strong opinion, without knowing all the facts about the caller, in my OPINION, is stupidity at its finest. But the public sucks it up. The failure to think a layer deeper about financial concepts is causing the transfer of thousands of dollars of your wealth.

Over the past twenty-five years, so-called modern

day financial planning has had mixed reviews. Lets face it, people become and continued to become millionaires long before financial planning became vogue. The thought of making millions by buying the right investments is right up there percentage wise with winning the lotto. Is there any correlation between financial planning over the last 25 years and the monetary predicament John Q. Public is in today? As Americans moved to investing in the markets, there also appeared larger sums of personal debt. Although the two are separate, it is all within the same time frame. What happened? Personal debt and bankruptcies and foreclosures are at an all time high and growing. Is it that personal income has not been able to keep pace with inflation and taxation? Possibly, increases in taxation have grown far greater than incomes. What happened? You would think that with all this professional financial help out there, the magazines, financial TV shows, investment brokers, and financial consultants (planners) that these problems wouldn't exist. Or have they created more problems than not in the last 25 years?

In order to improve your life you had to learn to change. You learn to eat differently to control your cholesterol. You learn to workout to stay in shape. You even learn to improve your golf game by taking lessons. All of these lessons require you to make changes in the way you used to do things. If you have a bad golf swing, buying a new driver won't improve your game (trust me on that one). Yet golf club manufacturers will always tell you different. Now what changes have you made financially? Banks and investment companies continue to insist that changing products, not your thinking, is your only solution to your financial problems.

TAX CUTS AND THE RICH

Another common misconception is that tax cuts are for the rich. This is nothing more than political "get-me-re-elected" talk. It is obvious that the rich make up such a small portion of the tax paying population, the politicians view this as a small group of voters. There are more poor, middle class, and upper middle class voters then there are rich voters. So don't be surprised when a politician favors the area where there are more voters. The tactic is as old as dirt. Divide and conquer, blame someone else for your problems, so you will vote for them. These are not poor or middle class people running for office. Remember, these people will spend millions to get elected to get a position that pays a couple of hundred thousand dollars a year. Makes sense, right?

I would like to compare our system of paying taxes to ten people going out to dinner. The common belief is the rich get more back than us ordinary tax payers and that is not fair. The reality is, the rich pay more so they <u>should</u> get more back.

If ten people went out to dinner, and when the bill came we used the rules of the tax code to pay this bill, it would look something like this: The bill for dinner for ten came to $100.00; Persons #1 through #4 would pay nothing; Person #5 would pay $1.00; Person #6 would pay $3.00; Person #7 would pay $7.00; Person #8 would pay $12.00; Person #9 would pay $18.00, and; Person #10 (the richest person) would pay $59.00.

If the restaurant owner decided to give the group a 20% discount. Now the dinner for 10 is only $80.00. How should they divide up the $20.00 savings? Remember, the first 4 paid nothing to begin with, so the savings should be divided between the remaining six. Twenty dollars divided by six equals $3.33 each. If you subtracted that amount from those six people's share, then persons #5 and #6 would be paid to eat their meals. This doesn't seem fair, so the equitable answer is to reduce each persons bill by the same percentage. The results look like this: Persons #1 through #5 would pay nothing; Person #6 would pay $2.00; Person #7 would pay $5.00; Person #8 would pay $9.00; Person #9 would pay $12.00; Person #10 (the richest person) would pay $52.00 instead of $59.00.

Now everyone starts comparing and complaining. Person #6 complains because he only got $1.00 back and Person #10 got $7.00 back. "Why should he get $7.00 back when I only got $2.00?" shouted person #7. "Why should the wealthy get all the breaks?" Person #1 through #4 yelled "We didn't get anything back. This system exploits the poor!" Then the nine people surrounded Person #10 and beat him up. That seemed to satisfy them. The next time they went out to dinner, Person #10 did not show up so they sat down and ate without him. When they were finished the bill came and they discovered they were $52.00 short.

The people who pay the highest taxes get the most benefit from a tax deduction. It's common sense math. If you tax them too much and attack them for being wealthy, they may decide not to show up at the table anymore. For everyone involved that would create an unintended consequence. Everyone would have to pay more.

DON'T LIMIT 401(k)
DEDUCTIONS TO
THE AMOUNT MATCHED...

I found the following sage advice in a local newspaper: Even though the company matches only part of the 401(k) contribution, it is to your benefit to put the most away in your 401(k) plan as you can, since 401(k) plans are an excellent way to save for retirement. The author of the article went on to profess that often many investors contribute only up to the company match within their 401(k) plan, and do not take advantage of their 401(k) plan if the company does not match, and he states that this is a mistake. He finalizes this train of thought by stating that with a 401(k) plan, an investor receives a double tax benefit. Not only is someone not taxed on contributions into a 401(k) plan, but all the income continues to grow on a tax deferred basis.

HALF THE STORY

These are the types of planning strategies we are presented with all the time. It is "surface thinking" at its simplest. I kept looking for the rest of the article that would tell the whole story and the truth. This was another example of someone deciding that the public didn't need to know the "rest of the story." They decided that it was not important to discuss the taxation issues of these strategies with the public.

Unintended Consequences:
Misguided Wisdom

The article should have concluded as follows: Although accumulating money for retirement should be everyone's goal, there are things that should be taken into consideration. A qualified plan simply defers the tax, as well as the tax <u>table</u>, to a later date. The assumption that you will retire to a lower tax bracket than the tax bracket you were in when you deposited the money is flawed. Studying the country's demographics, debt, and the history of the federal marginal tax bracket could lead you to the conclusion that it is very possible that you may retire to a higher tax bracket. If that is so, then the strategy of using a 401(k) as your main retirement savings vehicle may be a losing one. You are at the mercy of the Federal Government. When was the last time the government allowed you, as this planner cited, a double tax benefit without the ability to recoup those taxes, if not more, at a later date?

This article left a lot of questions unanswered. Failure to mention the effects of taxation on this 401(k) money could be considered an omission of the facts. Unintended consequences could result if you feel that taxes will go up in the future. I'm not saying all retirement plans are bad. I feel that when loading up or overloading qualified retirement plans and exposing yourself to future taxation, whatever level that may be, you should think at least twice about it. Once again, whose future are you financing, yours or the government's?

FEE-ONLY ADVISORS AND CONFLICTS OF INTEREST

I found more "wise" financial advice in a local periodical indicating that because of the pace of change in the market environment in tax laws and other areas, it is getting more difficult for the average person to manage their portfolio. Therefore, the idea of dealing with a professional makes sense. The author promoted the use of a fee-only advisor as opposed to a salesperson, since a true fee-only financial advisor will not have the conflict of interest inherent with commissioned salespeople.

As I mentioned previously, the investment industry has fought this battle for a long time. All too often planners want to put the client in the middle regarding the fee-based or commission question.

THERE IS A COST WHEN DEALING WITH GARBAGE, THERE IS A FEE FOR PICKING IT UP

The assumption that planners who charge their clients a fee to talk to them are the only planners who are professional and truly care about their clients, smells. I have had the opportunity to read and listen to such pompous ramblings. Along with losing investment picks, half-truth solutions and opinionists "wannabe" facts, they have the gall to charge client fees.

Make no mistake, a fee is no different than a commission. Fee-based planners would like us to assume that they are not motivated by money. Fees, commissions, and management and expense charges are all transfers of one's personal wealth. The "holier than thou" attitude assumes everyone who disagrees with them is not a professional. However, as an educator to students, clients and financial professionals, I have found that many of the sanctions against financial planners imposed by the SEC and NASD were and are against fee-based planners. You see, a crook is a crook. Bad fee-based planners and gouging commissioned planners make great cell mates.

More often than not, if I decide to wrestle with a skunk, I know I can win but I'll end up smelling funny. Remember, there are many professionals that charge fees. There are fees, sales charges, commissions and loads associated with every product a financial professional, whether fee-based or commissioned, promotes. How about some "no load, no fee" information?

WHY I DID THIS

I have included some of our seminar attendees comments. The basic ingredients in this book came form some of our educational seminars and college lectures. It is amazing to me how excited people get when they add a little knowledge to their financial lives. Hundreds of comments like these give me added support and inspiration. At the end of each session they are reminded to seek our professionals who understand the transfers of their wealth. It is my hope that with better understanding and some knowledge you will be able to make clearer and better decisions. Simply following the masses can create unintended consequences.

"A very interesting and enjoyable evening. You presented a compelling new perspective on finances and I left thinking about money differently."
Michael B., Publisher, Times Herald Newspapers

"A profound and life changing event. Thank you for a new life and lifestyle."
Reverend Joey H.

"Super job! A very enjoyable evening. Anyone who wants to make the most of their hard earned money should attend."
Dr. Margaret S., Chairperson and Associate Professor, Wayne State University School of Business

"Of the many financial services professionals with whom I have had the privilege to work with across the country, Renier & Associates has impressed me as being one of the finest. Leonard Renier has a tremendous ability to communicate the often difficult to understand financial concepts and make them easy for people to understand. Len is a very powerful and accomplished speaker who has spoken several times to our national audience at our national conventions. He has surrounded himself with advisors who like himself are not only competent but are serious about putting the wishes and goals of their clients first. Renier & Associates is a firm to which I can highly recommend clients looking for a quality advisor and financial service professionals who are looking for growing firm."
Don B., President, MoneyTrax Inc.

"You presented an extremely thought provoking seminar. I feel others would enjoy hearing your perspective on finances."

Cynthia B., Consumer Literacy Educator, Central Michigan University

"The understanding of wealth in America and the ability of the speakers to convey their understanding is dramatic. A great help for anyone interested in the dynamics of wealth. Concepts about demographics were helpful. Wealth transfer was unique and insightful."

Michael F., Mortgage banker

"Thought provoking- much to think about. Would recommend it to anyone who is serious about taking control of higher wealth."

E. W. G., Finance/ Management

"I definitely appreciate looking at the realities of finance in contrast to everything we've been taught in the past. Concepts sound good- always interested in learning about money."

Catherine B., Nurse anesthetist

"Very clear and easy to understand. Everyone should listen to this concept of utilizing transferred money."

Chet C., Dentist

"The rate of return on knowledge was incredible. Thanks for helping me think outside of my box."

Timothy N., Sales Manager

"Enjoyed everything. It was our first seminar and it was great!"

Judy C., Nurse

"Excellent. He made it possible to retire and live the life I wanted without any worries."
Don V., Engineer

"Great! It was a real eye opener!"
Al B., Promotions distributor

"I believe that you can help me to be free. I'm paying everyone and no one is paying me."
Terry L., Pipe fitter

"This was extremely rewarding and entertaining. I was very impressed with the information."
Valda A., Educator

"Very interesting. An hour and a half is not enough. Thank you for something to think about."
Marilyn G., Homemaker

"You presented excellent new information about mortgages and a interesting outlook on what we could expect in the near future."
Jerry J., Financial Services

"I was concerned that the subject matter would be beyond comprehension, but Mr. Renier delivered the topic excellently and I was wrong. The point of interest down the road is something most people don't take into consideration."
Carol B., Customer Service

"Very meaningful. You are helping me meet my goals."
Eva C., Health care director

"Very knowledgeable, peaked my interest in finding ways to increase my wealth."
Sheree O., Collateral Examiner

"Really insightful and thought-provoking."
Lionel E., Designer

"Very informative and eye opening, though somewhat depressing about how little I actually know!"
Venita K., Rehabilitation Counselor

"Awesome, eye opening. Left enough out to make me want more - lots of questions."
Jill B., Analyst, Ford Motor Credit

"I love your friendly approach to financial planning. It's the type of information we need the most, but least willing to learn about. Thank you for providing us avenues for financial freedom."
Beth J., Corporate Trainer

"Very enlightening. Thank you for the invite I really needed to be here."
Andrea S., Beautician

"Thought provoking and insightful! An awareness of financial planning like no other."
Robert W., Program Director

"I realize I am at the point of my life to make better choices about my investments. This seminar helped me feel much more optimistic about finding the right kind of help."
Mary N., Registered Nurse

"A very good example of the right approach to finances. This is an extremely important topic to anyone who wants to make more from their assets."
Michael M., IT Consultant

"Really peaked my interest. I learned a lot about a subject I knew very little about."
Chuck U., Quality Engineer

"Very timely concepts, especially considering the current state of the economy. Great use of specific examples."
Debbie J., Information Technology

"I am so glad that we had the opportunity to learn about the many benefits available to us now instead of later, especially as we get ready to buy our first home."
Cynthia G., Office Assistant

"Who knew? The light really came on (mortgage info and 401(K)s). I can't wait until the next one."
Mary W., Sales

"Good presentation and easily understood. Very useful information and interesting viewpoints."
Robert P., Chiropractor

"Such important information was discussed and taught at a level that anyone can understand. Only attend if your interested in control of your money."
Diane D., Marketing

"Excellent, very informative. This seminar offers a great method to personal financial freedom and wealth building."
Jeffrey W., System Administrator

"Extremely helpful, and really eye opening information. Would like to learn more."
Anne N., Window Treatment Designer

"Excellent! This was honestly the best financial seminar I have ever attended. Please let me know as to future seminars as I really want to 'grow my knowledge so I can grow my money!"
Pamela W., Attorney

"Good info, I hope it reaches the younger markets than me!"
Judy B., Retired

"Pertinent topic. A lot of content covered in a short time."
Brian B., Mortgage Lender

"Something everyone needs to hear. What a wake up call! Knowledgeable and entertaining."
Derek L., Program Coordinator

"Very informative. Good info and many good areas. Innovative and life changing ideas. The speaker was very emotional and enthusiastic."
Mary E., Opthamologist

"Great, a very impressive presentation."
Donald K., Accountant

"Very thorough. Relates very well to everyone and their finances."
Lesa L., Executive Assistant

"This guy is on the ball, he's great and he doesn't ask for anything in return."
Brad C., Cigar Producer

"Talked about things/ideas I had never heard from any other financial advisor. I am looking forward to working with Renier & Associates to better my wealth management."
Colleen T., Social Worker

"Good use of real life examples. Definately acheived goal of changing the way I thought about money."
Mario S., Attorney

"Intriguing. Very enlightening experience. Truly gets you thinking outside of the box."
Terry D., Information Technology

"Excellent, very dynamic. Thank you for the compelling presentation."
Heather W., Attorney

"Dynamic and captivating. Excellent speakers whose topics are appropriate for the time."
Arbrie G., Teacher

"The seminar was really enlightening. I was really frightened after September 11, 2001, but the speaker calmed me down. I will be attending future seminars."
Bernice B., Retired

"Very well presented and very enlightening. Very informative."
Russell B., Retired

"First seminar I've ever been to and I am glad I came. It was definitely worth my time."
Kim D., Homemaker

"I strongly recommend this seminar to anyone interested in making their money work for them."
Andrew H., Teacher

"I rate everything presented to me from topics to speakers eye opening and very interesting."
Robert C., Supervisor, General Motors

"Unbelievable, simple explanation of what our money can do when we know what taxes, interest and savings really cost. Simple 'CAN DO' things to do to use all of our money and most of all spend it on our family and ourselves."
Jerry H., Operations Manager/Engineer

"The talk was very informative and it does make me think very differently. It was a positive experience."
Diane H., Office Assistant

"This is info that everyone needs to know."
Judy R., Mortgage Banker

"Way to open your eyes on using your money to your advantage."
Jacqueline B., Art Director